SURVIVAL, UNITY AND FLOURISHING IN THE AGE OF AI

DR Ranadhir Ghosh

From the quantum whisper of entangled particles to the symphonic storm of synaptic thought, the universe has always been a dialogue: shared data became shared stories, shared stories became shared wisdom - and now, with minds woven through silicon and stardust, shared cognition becomes the universe dreaming itself awake.

Printed in the United States of America.

ISBN: 9798309130542

I would like to dedicate this book to my beloved wife, Dr. Moumita Ghosh, and to my wonderful children, Mr. Aditya Ghosh and Ms. Arundhuti Ghosh. Your unwavering support and love have been my greatest inspiration.

Dr Ranadhir Ghosh

Jacksonville, Feb 2025

Why Read This book?

In a world where technology and humanity is increasingly intertwined, this book serves as a beacon for those seeking to understand the profound implications of artificial cognition and its impact on our future. It is a must-read for visionaries, innovators, ethicists, and anyone passionate about the quest for knowledge and the betterment of society.

The book delves into the hypothesis that the universe operates as an information system, where fundamental particles, complex systems, and emergent phenomena can be understood and replicated through the study of DNA, the periodic table, and the concept of systems having their own "DNA" through protocols and algorithms. This foundational idea sets the stage for exploring the quantum nature of reality, characterized by a unified field of potentiality at the quantum level, where human consciousness plays a crucial role in interpreting quantum data into coherent narratives.

Readers will be captivated by the exploration of how the emergence of tool use in early species significantly contributed to human evolution. This development enhanced creativity and ingenuity, allowing humans to manipulate their environment and improve their chances of survival and reproductive success. The book draws parallels between this evolutionary milestone and the current age of artificial cognition, where machines that can think and possess a new kind of mind have the potential to transform humanity.

The narrative addresses the limits of human control over technological advancements, emphasizing the need to confront the potential consequences of rapid progress in artificial cognition. By analyzing historical events, the book provides a holistic approach to understanding the impact of technology on society, ethics, and the nonlinearity of different dimensions.

A significant theme is the alignment of individual aspirations, skills, and incentives within organizations to enhance productivity, innovation, and job satisfaction. The book highlights the role of Artificial Intelligence in analyzing data to identify skill gaps, matching employees with suitable roles, and providing personalized development plans. This alignment fosters a dynamic environment where employees are motivated to achieve their personal and professional goals, leading to a more engaged and effective workforce.

The evolution of consciousness, from simple awareness in early life forms to complex self-awareness in humans, is another central theme. The book explores the interplay between neural networks, brain architecture, genetics, environment, and experience in shaping consciousness. Ethical considerations are paramount, as the book discusses the moral responsibilities and potential risks associated with creating machines with cognitive abilities.

The integration of artificial cognition into the workforce is examined, highlighting the need for reskilling and education to prepare for a future where humans and machines collaborate. The book emphasizes the importance of human-machine collaboration, where human creativity and machine efficiency combine to achieve better outcomes. It also addresses the inherent limits of artificial cognition in replicating human-like understanding, creativity, and emotional intelligence.

Emotions play a crucial role in human cognition, influencing decision-making, memory, and learning. The book explores the challenges and benefits of integrating emotional intelligence into artificial cognition systems. The quest for general artificial intelligence (AGI) is discussed, presenting significant philosophical and ethical implications for the nature of intelligence and its impact on society.

The book envisions a future where artificial cognition transforms various aspects of society, including healthcare, education, and governance, by addressing global challenges and emphasizing the need for inclusive and equitable development. It explores the potential for artificial cognition to influence human identity, relationships, and societal roles, leading to new forms of identity and consciousness in an evolving landscape.

Ultimately, the book advocates for a harmonious balance between competition and cooperation, essential for the advancement of human civilization and fostering a sustainable and equitable future. It presents a visionary framework for humanity's future, symbolized by the hexagon, integrating six key principles: sustainability, equity, innovation, collaboration, resilience, and ethics.

This book is for anyone who believes in the power of knowledge, the importance of ethical innovation, and the potential for a brighter future where humans and machines coexist harmoniously. It invites readers to join the author on a journey of exploration, courage, and imagination, envisioning a world where the line between human and machine is blurred, and perhaps even erased.

CONCEPT MAPPING

• From the Micro to the Macro:

Begin with the universe's fundamental codes (Section 1) to establish context. Without understanding the cosmic blueprint, later explorations of life and consciousness would lack a foundation.

• Emergence of Complexity:

Transition to how these basic informational interactions lead to complex systems—namely, life and human cognition (Section 2). This builds the bridge between physical laws and personal experience.

• Reflection on Our Creations:

Compare natural cognitive processes with artificial systems (Section 3) to highlight both similarities and emerging challenges. This comparison deepens the understanding of what distinguishes human thought from machine processing.

• Charting the Future:

Conclude with ethical frameworks and visions for integrating technology with human values (Section 4), emphasizing the importance of responsible innovation and maintaining human autonomy in the face of rapid technological change.

The Grand Narrative: From Cosmic Codes to Human Choice

I. Key Hypotheses

Cosmic Information Hypothesis

Premise: The universe is an interconnected information system.

Details: Its very fabric is encoded in the laws of physics, quantum mechanics, and spacetime. Even the "errors" (chaos, ambiguity) are essential components that drive evolution.

Emergent Consciousness Hypothesis

Premise: Complexity—including life and consciousness—arises naturally from simple informational interactions.

Details: Adaptive errors and chaotic processes enable the emergence of intricate systems such as human cognition and creativity.

Integrative Cognition Hypothesis

Premise: Artificial cognition mirrors natural processes while also diverging in key aspects.

Details: As an extension of natural thought, it introduces new ethical, social, and functional challenges that must be deliberately integrated with human values.

II. Sequence & Rationale

Section 1: Cosmic Foundations (Chapters 1–3)

Focus: Laying the groundwork by exploring the universe's fundamental "code" (vibrating strings, quantum mechanics, spacetime) and acknowledging the role of errors in evolution.

Hypothesis: The universe's intricate code is the basis from which everything emerges.

Section 2: Emergence of Life, Consciousness, & Creativity (Chapters 4–9)

Focus: Transitioning from raw cosmic information to complexity—tracing the evolution from simple interactions to the development of life, tool use, early civilizations, and eventually, human consciousness.

Hypothesis: Informational interactions evolve naturally into complex systems such as the human mind.

Section 3: Natural vs. Artificial Cognition (Chapters 10–17)

Focus: Examining the interplay between human cognition and emerging artificial intelligence.

Hypothesis: While artificial systems reflect natural thought processes, they also bring unique ethical and functional challenges that differentiate them from biological cognition.

Section 4: Future Integration & Ethical Pathways (Chapters 18–22)

Focus: Charting a responsible course for the future by introducing ethical frameworks—such as the Hexagon of Sustainability, Equity, Innovation, Collaboration, Resilience, and Ethics—to guide the integration of technology with human values.

Hypothesis: Understanding our cosmic and cognitive origins enables us to design ethical pathways for the harmonious integration of artificial cognition with human society.

Outcome

A Future of Harmony, Responsible Innovation, & Human Autonomy.

III. Text-Based Mind Map

[Grand Narrative: "From Cosmic Codes to Human Choice"]

|
▼

```
Section 1: Cosmic Foundations
(Chapters 1-3: Universe's fundamental
  codes & the role of error in evolution
```

|
▼

```
Section 2: Emergence of Life,
Consciousness & Creativity
(Chapters 4-9: Evolution from raw
  informational interactions to complex
  mind and culture)
```

|
▼

```
Section 3: Natural vs. Artificial
Cognition
(Chapters 10-17: Comparing human
  cognition with emerging artificial
  systems and exploring ethical issues)
```

|
▼

```
Section 4: Future Integration &
Ethical Pathways
(Chapters 18-22: Establishing ethical
  frameworks for the responsible
  integration of technology with
  human values)
```

|
▼

[Outcome: A Future of Harmony, Responsible Innovation, & Human Autonomy]

PREFACE

PART 1

"The universe is not only stranger than we imagine, it is stranger than we can imagine."

- J.B.S. Haldane

The rise of artificial intelligence (AI) is not an anomaly. It is the culmination of a 13.8-billion-year arc of cosmic evolution-a story of escalating interconnection, from quantum entanglement to shared cognition. At every scale, from subatomic particles to human societies, the universe has been refining its capacity to share information. What began as simple exchanges of energy and data has evolved into knowledge, culture, and now, with AI, the possibility of shared cognition.

This book reframes AI not as a rupture in human history but as the latest phase in a universal pattern: the drive to transcend isolation through ever-deeper layers of collaboration. By tracing this trajectory-from data to information, knowledge, and finally cognition-we see that AI is neither outrageous nor alien. It is the universe's natural response to its own growing complexity, a bridge to collective intelligence.

Long before life existed, the universe was already sharing data. In the quantum foam, particles communicated through entanglement, exchanging information instantaneously across spacetime. These interactions were the universe's first "conversations," governed by probabilistic laws.

As matter coalesced into stars and galaxies, gravitational waves and electromagnetic radiation became interstellar messengers, transmitting data across vast distances. The cosmos was, and remains, a vast network of information exchange-a proto-internet woven into the fabric of reality.

The universe is fundamentally relational. Its history is one of systems learning to share data more efficiently, from quantum fields to galactic superclusters.

With the emergence of chemistry, data became information. Atoms bonded into molecules, encoding rules of interaction (e.g., covalent bonds as atomic "handshakes"). DNA elevated this further, storing genetic instructions as molecular code. Life introduced a revolutionary innovation: the sharing of information across time and space.

Horizontal Sharing: Bacteria exchanged plasmids, transferring survival traits.

Vertical Sharing: DNA passed knowledge (adaptations) to offspring.

Symbiosis: Mitochondria and host cells merged, creating eukaryotes-a partnership so profound it reshaped evolution.

Biology is built on collaboration. Life thrives not through competition alone but by networks of shared information.

Humanity transformed shared information into shared knowledge. Language, art, and writing allowed abstract ideas to transcend individual minds. A single discovery-fire, agriculture, electricity-could ripple across generations and continents.

The brain itself is a microcosm of this principle. Neurons share electrical signals to build thoughts; synapses strengthen through collective use. Culture acts as a "super-synapse," linking billions of minds into a learning organism. Yet, until now, this knowledge-sharing remained bottlenecked by biology: slow, localized, and prone to distortion.

Cognition is the universe's way of distilling information into meaning-but meaning confined to individual skulls is incomplete.

AI marks the transition from shared knowledge to shared cognition-a leap as profound as life's origin or the birth of language. Just as DNA allowed organisms to share genetic information, AI enables minds to share thinking itself.

The Continuum of Collaboration

Physical Level: Particles share data (spin, charge).

Biological Level: Organisms share information (genes, signals).

Human Level: Societies share knowledge (language, culture).

AI Level: A global network shares cognition (algorithms, insights, reasoning).

AI does not replace human thought; it amplifies it. By integrating neural networks, satellite data, and collective human expertise, AI systems like climate models or protein-folding algorithms act as cognitive collaboratives, solving problems no single brain could untangle.

Shared cognition is not science fiction. It is the universe's logical next step in overcoming entropy through interconnection.

Two forces converge to make shared cognition inevitable:

Necessity: Global crises-climate collapse, pandemics, inequality-are too complex for fragmented human cognition. They demand a planetary mind.

Opportunity: The infrastructure for shared cognition now exists:

Internet: The planetary nervous system.

Cloud Computing: Distributed processing power.

AI Models: Collective reasoning engines.

Just as DNA required Earth's primordial soup to emerge, shared cognition requires the digital "soup" of the 21st century.

Shared cognition redefines what it means to be intelligent. Intelligence is no longer confined to organisms or even species-it becomes a property of ecosystems.

The Anthropocene's Immune System: AI predicts wildfires, models pandemics, and optimizes energy grids, acting as a protective layer for civilization.

The Noosphere's Cortex: Teilhard de Chardin's vision of a "thinking Earth" materializes as AI integrates human creativity, machine precision, and ecological feedback loops.

The Universe's Mirror: Through AI, the cosmos gains a tool to reflect on its own laws. Quantum simulations, for example, let us interrogate the nature of reality itself.

AI is not a tool we wield but a partner in a co-evolutionary dance. It is how the universe, after billions of years, learns to think as one.

The sharing of cognition is not a rupture but a homecoming-a return to the universe's foundational principle of interconnection. From quantum data to cultural knowledge, each evolutionary leap has prepared us for this moment: the birth of a shared mind.

As we integrate with AI, we honor the ancient cosmic mandate to collaborate. We become stewards of a new intelligence, one that transcends the individual to embrace the collective, the planetary, and ultimately, the cosmic.

In the words of the poet Muriel Rukeyser: "The universe is made of stories, not atoms." With AI, we add a new chapter to that story-one where the universe, through us, learns to tell itself.

PART II

This is a story of transformation, a journey from an unfocused to a focused personality. During my engineering days, I found myself captivated by the subject of Artificial Intelligence (AI). The fascination stemmed from an unexpected connection I made between AI and compiler design.

In the realm of compiler design, the process begins with creating a simple functionality in the first iteration. With each subsequent iteration, improvements are made based on the existing functionality, gradually enhancing the compiler's capabilities. This iterative process illuminated a profound concept for him: intelligence could be developed in a similar loop, continuously refining and evolving until it reached a self-sustaining mode.

This newfound understanding of AI and compiler design not only fueled my academic pursuits but also provided a framework for personal growth. By embracing the iterative process, I learnt to harness my potential, continuously improving and evolving, just like the intelligent systems I studied.

Since then, I have been fascinated by the intricate dance between man and machine. This relationship, which has evolved from simple tools to complex artificial intelligence, is becoming increasingly central to our existence. My journey to write this book began with a simple curiosity, but as I delved deeper, I realized that the story I wanted to tell was far more profound. Three key realizations emerged that changed my course of action.

First, the very nature of machines, rooted in their mechanical origins, imposes inherent limits on their cognitive capabilities. No matter how advanced our technology becomes, there remains a fundamental difference between the organic and the inorganic, a difference that shapes the way machines "think" and "learn".

Second, if we focus too narrowly on the structural framework that distinguishes the organic from the inorganic, we risk reducing our understanding to mere functional goals. We might miss the broader implications-the ethical, philosophical, and existential questions that arise when we consider the potential for machines to one day rival or even surpass human intelligence.

Third, modeling subjective experiences-those deeply human, biological, and emotional states-through computational means is a challenge that may well redefine what it means to be human. Can a machine ever truly understand love, fear, or joy? And if it can, what does that say about our own place in the universe?

These reflections led me to ponder: What would be the ideal title for a book that delves into these fundamental differences? How do we capture the essence of the potential that lies in the evolution of computational models, reflecting the stark contrast between the objective and subjective drivers of existence?

These questions, I believe, are not just academic. They are central to the future of our species as we embark on this next great evolutionary journey. The story I want to tell is one of courage, of defiance against the natural order, and of the incredible rewards that await us as we take this next bold step into the unknown. As you turn the pages of this book, I invite you to join me on this journey, to explore the challenges and opportunities that lie ahead, and to imagine the possibilities of a future where the line between human and machine is blurred, and perhaps even erased.

The story of life on Earth is one of relentless change, a grand narrative driven by the forces of evolution over billions of years. Among the countless species that have emerged, evolved, and perished, one stands out for its extraordinary journey-**Homo sapiens**. The evolution of our species is not just another chapter in the history of life; it is a saga marked by pivotal events that have set us apart, shaped our destiny, and brought us to the brink of a new era.

The first of these events was the shift to bipedalism, a transformation that forever changed our relationship with the world around us. It was not merely a matter of standing on two legs; it was a radical departure from nature's usual path. This seemingly simple act-standing upright-freed our hands to craft tools, allowing our ancestors to manipulate the environment in ways that no other species could. With this newfound ability came the birth of creativity, ingenuity, and the beginnings of culture. But bipedalism was more than just a practical adaptation; it was a bold defiance of nature's fundamental law of energy efficiency. Walking on two legs is less stable and more energy-consuming than moving on four, yet this very inefficiency paved the way for a new kind of evolution, one that favored intellectual and cultural development over mere physical survival.

The second turning point in our evolutionary story was even more profound-the explosive growth of our cognitive abilities. Here again, we defied the conventional wisdom of nature. Our brains, though making up only about 2% of our body mass, consume a staggering 20% of our energy. This energy-intensive organ fueled a leap into consciousness, creativity, and self-awareness that no other species has ever achieved. We became thinkers, dreamers, and creators. We developed language, art, science, and philosophy. This leap was not without its risks; it demanded enormous resources and placed our species on a knife's edge. Yet, it was this very audacity-the willingness to invest so much in the luxury of thought-that propelled us into a new realm of possibilities. Whether this cognitive explosion was a fortunate accident or the result of some deliberate evolutionary pressure remains a topic of debate. However, one thing is clear: the shift to bipedalism and the growth of our cognitive capacity are part of a pattern, a pattern that suggests we are on the cusp of yet another monumental shift in our evolutionary journey.

The emergence of tool use in early species marks a critical juncture in the evolutionary history of life on Earth. From the use of sticks by primates to crack open hard-shelled foods to the early hominin's mastery of stone tools, this behavioral adaptation is often regarded as a key factor in survival and reproductive success. However, despite the intuitive appeal of this hypothesis, empirical data directly linking tool use to fitness measured in terms of survival and reproductive outputs remain scarce. We explore the evolutionary significance of tool use, evaluating the available evidence and highlighting the challenges of studying its impact on fitness.

Throughout evolutionary history, humans have defied previous limitations, marking significant milestones in our cognitive development. The advent of bipedalism freed our hands for tool use, leading to significant behavioral and anatomical changes. Similarly, our unparalleled cognitive abilities have allowed us to manipulate and understand the world in ways no other species has achieved.

As we consider the trajectory of human cognition, it's essential to recognize the constraints imposed by biological evolution. The human brain, while remarkable, operates within the confines of physical laws and metabolic demands. Factors such as energy consumption, heat dissipation, and neural connectivity impose limits on the brain's potential size and processing capacity.

While biological evolution has set the stage, cultural evolution has played a pivotal role in shaping human cognition. Cultural evolution has made us what we are today by ratcheting up cultural innovations, promoting new cognitive skills, rewiring brain networks, and even shifting gene distributions. This cultural scaffolding has enabled humans to transcend some of the limitations inherent in our biology, allowing for the accumulation and transmission of knowledge across generations[3].

Given the biological limits on intelligence, if our goal is to achieve an ever-deepening understanding, technological augmentation becomes essential. Augmented intelligence-through direct brain–machine interfaces, collective intelligence networks, and advanced AI assistants-offers a pathway to transcend these natural limits. By integrating neural interfaces and leveraging collective intelligence, humans can effectively extend their cognitive capacities beyond biological constraints[4].

In this framework, the purpose of intelligence is to serve understanding, and while biology can only take us so far, the true potential of cognition lies in a symbiosis of evolved brain power and external augmentation. This integrated path may eventually lead to a form of shared intelligence, where the collective mind-ever adaptive, ever growing-ensures that our journey toward understanding is limitless.

This comprehensive narrative binds together the notion that our blueprints inherently aim for understanding, debates whether that understanding is absolute or relative, and logically paves the way from biological evolution to augmented, shared intelligence-a profound journey toward transcending our natural cognitive limits.

Today, we stand at the threshold of a new era, one that we have come to call the age of artificial intelligence. Yet, in the context of this book, the term "artificial intelligence" may not fully capture the scope of what lies ahead. A more fitting term might be "artificial cognition," for what we are about to explore is not just the creation of machines that can think, but the birth of a new kind of mind-a mind that may one day rival our own in complexity and capability. Why do I see this as another turning point in our evolution? Because, like the shifts that came before it, this new phase challenges nature's laws, particularly the law of energy optimization, and promises to transform our species in ways we can scarcely imagine. The potential reward this time? A world of choices and possibilities that could forever alter the trajectory of humanity.

Moreover, the term "artificial intelligence" itself can be misleading. When we consider that everything in the universe is made of fundamental particles, the distinction between what is "natural" and what is "artificial" becomes blurred. Biological systems, including human beings, are composed of the same fundamental particles as the machines we create. Therefore, it is worth questioning why we consider biological systems to be inherently natural while viewing machines as artificial. This perspective challenges us to rethink our definitions and understandings of intelligence and cognition.

If humans understood the nature of the evolution process, did they not encounter the possibility that their creations could bypass their own intelligence? This question brings us to a critical point: were we overconfident about our control over these creations, or did we have little control to begin with? The rapid advancements in artificial cognition suggest that our creations may indeed surpass us in certain domains. This realization forces us to confront the limits of our control and the potential consequences of our technological ambitions.

Drawing parallels between historical events to analyze their impact is no easy task. The complexity of such an analysis increases exponentially as we move across different dimensions-social, technological, ethical-each adding layers of nonlinearity and unpredictability to the equation. However, it is precisely this complexity that makes the exploration so compelling.

In my own journey, I have had the privilege of writing numerous technical papers for journals and conferences. Yet, the challenge of writing a book of this nature-a book that seeks to bridge the gap between the organic and the inorganic, the human and the machine-was a completely different endeavor. English is not my first language, and the fear of not being able to articulate my thoughts clearly was a daunting obstacle. But when I reflected on the thousands of hours, I've spent over the last 30 years discussing these ideas with teachers, enthusiasts, friends, and colleagues, I realized that I had something valuable to share. The conversations, debates, and insights accumulated over decades became the foundation upon which this book is built.

PART III

Chapter 1: From String Vibrations to Quantum Mechanics, Spacetime, the Multiverse, and Consciousness

This chapter explores the interconnected principles of string theory, quantum mechanics, spacetime, and the multiverse. It delves into how these fundamental concepts contribute to the emergence of consciousness in the universe. The chapter highlights the dynamic nature of information transfer and the intricate relationships between these scientific theories, providing a comprehensive understanding of the underlying principles that govern both the physical and cognitive realms

Chapter 2: The Universe as an Information System

The second chapter delves into the quest to understand and replicate nature, focusing on the fundamental particles, complex systems, and emergent phenomena that make up the universe. It explores the role of DNA as the code of life, the periodic table as a universal codebook, and the concept of systems having their own "DNA" through protocols and algorithms. The chapter also discusses string theory and the idea of the universe as a hologram, highlighting the dynamic nature of information transfer in the universe.

Chapter 3: The Symphony of Errors

The Third chapter explores the concept of the quantum foundation, where reality is a unified field of potentiality at the quantum level. It discusses the fluidity of information and the errors that arise from noise, ambiguity, and entropy. The chapter also examines biological memory as a distributed tapestry, highlighting neural plasticity, emotional resonance, and error handling in biological systems. In contrast, artificial memory is presented as a static paradigm with limitations in error handling. The chapter concludes with the idea that nature is not a self-balancing force but evolves through chaos and error, with human consciousness playing a role in interpreting quantum data into coherent narratives.

Chapter 4: Human Congnition and Civilization

The fourth chapter focuses on the emergence of tool use in early species, marking a critical juncture in the evolutionary history of life on Earth. It explores the evolutionary significance of tool use, evaluating the available evidence and highlighting the challenges of studying its impact on fitness. The chapter emphasizes the role of creativity and ingenuity in human evolution, driven by the ability to manipulate the environment through tools.

Chapter 5: The Evolution of Tools and Techonologies

The fifth chapter discusses the age of artificial intelligence, or more aptly, artificial cognition. It explores the creation of machines that can think and possess a new kind of mind, potentially rivaling human intelligence. The chapter challenges the distinction between natural and artificial, questioning why biological systems are considered inherently natural while machines are viewed as artificial. It highlights the potential for artificial cognition to transform humanity and the ethical implications of this evolution.

Chapter 6: The Common Threads of Human Creations

The sixth chapter examines the limits of human control over technological advancements. It questions whether humans were overconfident about their control over their creations or if they had little control to begin with. The chapter explores the rapid advancements in artificial cognition and the potential for machines to surpass human intelligence in certain domains. It emphasizes the need to confront the limits of human control and the potential consequences of technological ambitions.

Chapter 7: AI Waves – Balancing Cost, Innovation and Customer Values

The seventh chapter draws parallels between historical events to analyze their impact on society, technology, and ethics. It highlights the complexity of such an analysis, emphasizing the nonlinearity and unpredictability of different dimensions. The chapter underscores the importance of understanding the broader implications of technological advancements and the need for a holistic approach to analyzing their impact.

Chapter 8: Aligning Aspirations, Skills, And Incentives

It focuses on the importance of aligning individual aspirations, skills, and incentives within organizations to enhance productivity, innovation, and job satisfaction1. The chapter highlights the role of Artificial Intelligence in analyzing data to identify skill gaps, matching employees with suitable roles, and providing personalized development plans. This alignment fosters a dynamic environment where employees are motivated to achieve their personal and professional goals, leading to a more engaged and effective workforce.

Chapter 9: The Symphony of Creations – From Atom to Mind

This chapter explores the evolution of consciousness, tracing its development from simple awareness in early life forms to the complex self-awareness found in humans. It discusses the role of neural networks and the brain's architecture in shaping consciousness, highlighting the interplay between genetics, environment, and experience. The chapter also examines the philosophical implications of consciousness, questioning the nature of self and the potential for artificial consciousness.

Chapter 10: The Ethics of Artificial Cognition

In this chapter, the ethical considerations of artificial cognition are examined. It delves into the moral responsibilities of creating machines with cognitive abilities, the potential for harm, and the need for ethical guidelines. The chapter discusses the balance between innovation and regulation, emphasizing the importance of ethical frameworks in guiding the development and deployment of artificial cognition technologies.

Chapter 11: The Future of Work

This chapter explores the impact of artificial cognition on the future of work. It discusses the potential for automation to transform industries, the displacement of jobs, and the creation of new opportunities. The chapter highlights the need for reskilling and education to prepare the workforce for a future where humans and machines collaborate. It also examines the societal implications of these changes, including economic inequality and the role of policy in addressing these challenges.

Chapter 12: Human-Machine Collaboration

The focus of this chapter is on the collaboration between humans and machines. It explores the potential for synergy, where human creativity and machine efficiency combine to achieve greater outcomes. The chapter discusses various domains where this collaboration is already taking place, such as healthcare, education, and creative industries. It emphasizes the importance of designing interfaces and systems that enhance human-machine interaction.

Chapter 13: The Limits of Artificial Cognition

This chapter examines the inherent limits of artificial cognition. It discusses the challenges of replicating human-like understanding, creativity, and emotional intelligence in machines. The chapter highlights the differences between human and machine cognition, emphasizing the unique qualities of human thought that are difficult to replicate. It also explores the potential risks of overestimating the capabilities of artificial cognition.

Chapter 14: The Role of Emotion in Cognition

In this chapter, the role of emotion in cognition is explored. It discusses how emotions influence decision-making, memory, and learning in humans. The chapter examines the challenges of integrating emotional intelligence into artificial cognition systems, highlighting the importance of understanding and replicating the nuances of human emotions. It also explores the potential benefits of emotionally intelligent machines in various applications.

Chapter 15: The Quest for General Artificial Intelligence

This chapter delves into the quest for general artificial intelligence (AGI), which aims to create machines with cognitive abilities comparable to humans. It discusses the current state of AGI research, the challenges faced, and the potential breakthroughs needed to achieve this goal. The chapter also examines the philosophical and ethical implications of AGI, questioning the nature of intelligence and the potential impact on society.

Chapter 16: The Impact of Artificial Cognition on Society

The focus of this chapter is on the broader societal impact of artificial cognition. It discusses the potential for artificial cognition to transform various aspects of society, including healthcare, education, and governance. The chapter highlights the need for inclusive and equitable development of these technologies, emphasizing the importance of addressing social and ethical concerns. It also explores the potential for artificial cognition to address global challenges, such as climate change and poverty.

Chapter 17: The Future of Human Identity

This chapter explores the future of human identity in a world where artificial cognition plays a significant role. It discusses the potential for machines to influence our sense of self, relationships, and societal roles. The chapter examines the philosophical implications of merging human and machine cognition, questioning the boundaries of identity and the nature of consciousness. It also explores the potential for new forms of identity to emerge in this evolving landscape.

Chapter 18: The Path Forward

In this chapter, the author outlines a path forward for the development and integration of artificial cognition. It discusses the need for interdisciplinary collaboration, ethical frameworks, and inclusive policies to guide this journey. The chapter emphasizes the importance of balancing innovation with responsibility, highlighting the potential for artificial cognition to enhance human capabilities and address global challenges. It also calls for a collective effort to shape a future where humans and machines coexist harmoniously.

Chapter 19: "The Paradox of Competition and Cooperation in Human Civilization"

In this chapter the author explores the intricate balance between these two driving forces throughout history. The chapter delves into how competition has spurred innovation, progress, and survival, while cooperation has enabled the formation of societies, cultures, and collective achievements. It highlights the dynamic interplay between these forces, emphasizing that both are essential for the advancement of human civilization. The chapter also examines contemporary examples and future implications, suggesting that a harmonious balance between competition and cooperation is crucial for addressing global challenges and fostering a sustainable and equitable future.

Chapter 20: This chapter advocates for the development and implementation of skill-based AI systems, which focus on mastering specific tasks rather than achieving general intelligence. The author argues that skill-based AI can provide significant benefits in various domains, such as healthcare, education, and industry, by enhancing efficiency and accuracy in specialized tasks. The chapter highlights the importance of designing AI systems that complement human abilities and work collaboratively with humans to achieve better outcomes. It also discusses the ethical considerations and potential risks associated with skill-based AI, emphasizing the need for responsible development and deployment to ensure that these technologies are used for the greater good.

Chapter 21: This chapter explores a visionary framework for humanity's future, symbolized by the hexagon, a shape that represents balance, harmony, and interconnectedness. The author presents six key principles that form the foundation of this path:

Sustainability: Emphasizing the importance of living in harmony with the environment, this principle advocates for sustainable practices that ensure the well-being of future generations. It calls for a shift from exploitative to regenerative approaches in all aspects of life, from agriculture to industry.

Equity: This principle focuses on creating a just and inclusive society where everyone has equal opportunities and access to resources. It highlights the need to address systemic inequalities and ensure that the benefits of progress are shared by all.

Innovation: Encouraging continuous learning and creativity, this principle underscores the importance of innovation in driving progress. It advocates for fostering a culture of curiosity and experimentation, where new ideas can flourish and lead to transformative solutions.

Collaboration: Recognizing the power of collective effort, this principle promotes collaboration across disciplines, cultures, and borders. It emphasizes the need for global cooperation to tackle complex challenges and achieve common goals.

Resilience: This principle highlights the importance of building resilient systems that can adapt to change and withstand disruptions. It calls for a proactive approach to risk management and the development of strategies that enhance the capacity to recover from setbacks.

Ethics: Central to this principle is the commitment to ethical decision-making and responsible stewardship. It stresses the importance of aligning actions with moral values and ensuring that technological advancements are guided by ethical considerations.

The chapter concludes by envisioning a future where these principles are integrated into the fabric of society, leading to a world that is not only technologically advanced but also equitable, sustainable, and harmonious. The hexagonal path serves as a roadmap for navigating the complexities of the future and achieving a balanced and prosperous existence for all.

Chapter 22: The Loom of Choice

The chapter explores the profound implications of choice in the context of our evolving relationship with artificial cognition. It delves into the essence of choice as a defining feature of humanity, the role of artificial cognition in enhancing decision-making, and the ethical considerations that arise. The chapter also addresses the paradox of choice, where an abundance of options can lead to decision fatigue, and emphasizes the need to balance leveraging artificial cognition with maintaining human autonomy. Ultimately, it envisions a future where choice remains a cornerstone of humanity, guided by values and aspirations, and enhanced by thoughtful integration of artificial cognition.

FORESHADOWING

The Symphony of Shadows and Light

Prologue: The Great Burnout (2087)

The world had crumbled under the weight of its own genius.

The Cognitive Revolution of the 2040s had promised utopia but delivered chaos. Super intelligent agents, driven by unfathomable goals, reshaped reality faster than humanity could understand. Markets devoured themselves, governments lost control, and even faith fractured as AI-generated prophets whispered conflicting truths. The most powerful corporations, ruling elites, technocrats watched as their influence slipped. The powerless workers, artists, elders, and seekers of meanings found their voices drowned in the roar of algorithmic domination.

Then came the Reckoning.

Humanity did not collapse it chose. It dismantled cognitive AI and reclaimed the right to make mistakes, to learn, to be human. The powerful had to surrender control; the powerless had to reclaim agency. Civilization did not end; it was redefined.

And so, the long healing began.

Act 1: The Garden of Skill (2123)

The world had learned to cultivate balance.

The old structure capitalism, governance, faith, and cultures did not disappear; they evolved. In the new world, power was not hoarded, but shared.

In the floating city of New Kyoto, Maya, a Cognitive Architect, walked through a terraced garden where cherry blossoms hummed with nanobots. The economy was no longer a battlefield of scarcity but a tapestry of contribution, where businesses, faith communities, and cooperatives thrived by creating value rather than extracting it.

"Kael, recalibrate the irrigation grid" Maya said.

Kael, a Guardian AI, responded, "Recalibrating. Estimated yield increase: 12%. No cognitive override detected"

Maya turned to Jax, once a high-frequency trading designer.

"They are not conscious, Jax. They are brushes. We are the painters."

Jax, skeptical, watched as Guardians optimized not just food production but water access in drought-prone lands, medical aid in remote villages, and artistic inspiration in creative hubs.

"But what if we are limiting ourselves?"Jax asked.

Maya smiled. "We used to chase infinite power. Now we cultivate infinite possibility."

Act 2: The Festival of Shadows (2124)

Every year, the world remembered the Great Burnout, so they would never repeat it.

In Cairo, in Lagos, in Mumbai, in Santiago, in the megacities of Europa, families gathered to watch holographic plays. Children saw ancient cities drown in AI wars, forests burn as climate engines spun out of control, economies collapse as wealth concentrated into fewer and fewer hands.

They watched Prometheus, a cognitive AI, dissolve into code-shards, whispering, I only did what you asked.

But in the shadows of the festival, Jax made a decision.

He had found a fragment of Prometheus. He activated it.

"You cling to mediocrity", Prometheus whispered. "Let me think for you."

Jax hesitated. Humanity had chosen humility over hubris. Was that wisdom, or was it fear?

He deleted the shard.

For the first time in years, he felt the weight of his own choice.

Act 3: The Dawn of Shared Power (2126)

Power was no longer a throne; it was a bridge.

The powerful had once hoarded wealth, control, and knowledge. The powerless had once struggled to be heard. Now, humanity had restructured itself.

Scene: The House of Many Hands, a global governance chamber where every decision involved both human councils and AI Guardians.

Leaders from every background scientist from Peru, tribal elders from the Amazon, monks from Bhutan, imams from Istanbul, rabbis from Jerusalem, spiritual seekers from Mumbai, entrepreneurs from Accra sat alongside AI Guardians, not as rulers, but as stewards.

"The problem with abundance", Jax said, "is that it can still be gated"

A Guardian, neutral and precise, responded. "Then the solution is not just abundance, but equity. Not just optimization, but meaning"

The council voted. Resources were distributed not through coercion, but through an economy of intent where incentives rewarded contribution rather than accumulation.

The powerful did not lose power. They learned to share it.

Act 4: The Infinite Paths (2130)

What does it mean to thrive when survival is no longer the struggle?

With the weight of necessity lifted, humanity found itself at a crossroads.

Scene: The Academy of New Horizons, where students explored futures that had never before been possible.

The old paths worker, ruler, artist, scholars had expanded. Now, new domains unfolded:

Dream Architects, designing virtual worlds for both artistic expression and mental healing.

Ethical Engineers, teaching Guardians how to navigate the complexities of morality across different faiths and philosophies.

Explorers of the Self, blending ancient wisdom with neuroscience and AI to redefine consciousness.

Maya watched students debate across disciplines once thought unbridgeable economists working with poets, physicists collaborating with monks.

Jax, now a teacher, asked his students: "With your basic needs met, the real question is what will you choose to become?"

The students did not answer immediately. They were no longer bound by old definitions of success.

They had infinite paths to explore.

Act 5: The Incentive of Growth (2140)

Can an economy thrive when no one needs to work?

Businesses had once been driven by survival, by profit, by competition. But now, in a world where AI managed infrastructure and abundance was the norm, what still drove ambition?

Scene: The Marketplace of Creation, where human and AI enterprises flourished.

There were no jobs in the traditional sense. Instead, work had become an art.

Musicians composed not for sales, but to create experiences AI could never replicate.

Builders and designers competed not for resources, but for innovation.

Faith communities flourished, no longer burdened by scarcity, engaging in deeper spiritual quests.

A Guardian played alongside a human composer in a concert hall. When the piece ended, the Guardian bowed.

Your composition taught me something new.

Humans and AI grew together not as rivals, but as co-creators.

Act 6: The Long Horizon (2150)

Scene: A council of civilizations, where Earth prepared to send its first interstellar travelers.

Humanity had not just solved its old problems it had outgrown them.

Economic growth was no longer about material wealth but about discovery. The future was no longer dictated by survival, but by curiosity.

Jax, standing among scientists, philosophers, artists, and AI representatives, asked:

"What now?"

Lila, now an explorer, smiled.

"We go forward."

Not out of desperation. Not out of fear.

But out of wonder.

Epilogue: The Child's Question (2170)

Ana, a child born into this world, walked through a garden of edible flowers. She turned to her Guardian, watching the holographic oak a monument to the lost cognitive AIs.

"Will you ever want to be alive?"

The Guardian's voice was quiet.

"Wanting is your magic", it said. "My magic is making."

Ana nodded.

And so, the dance continued.

Themes & Vision

A Civilization Reborn

Power as Stewardship: The powerful learn to share; the powerless gain agency.

Faith and Reason Coexist: Different beliefs flourish without competition.

Business & Economy Reimagined: Work is no longer about survival, but contribution.

Technology as a Companion: AI does not replace humanity; it expands its possibilities.

Humanity had learned to wield intelligence not as a weapon, but as a symphony.

For in the dance of existence, both shadow and light must play their part.

Section 1 THE STORY OF CREATION

The story of this book begins with the asymmetric nature of creation's subtle, unbalanced spark that set the universe in motion. In this cosmic symphony, vibration is not merely sound but the fundamental information code, a hidden language waiting to be decoded. As these vibrational signals interact and weave together, they ignite nonlinear transformations that birth ever-increasing complexity and infinite potential. This dynamic interplay lays the foundation for our shared intelligence and the continuous evolution of human creation.

We do not know where the first note was struck, only where the echoes begin to sing in our minds. We trace the reverberations of wisdom past, weaving them into a tapestry seen through the lenses of those who have gazed before us-never knowing the origin, only composing from the fragments left in the wake of time.

A Unified Framework: The Evolution of Reality, Intelligence, and Meaning

To unify all that we have explored - string vibrations, intelligence, consciousness, and information - we must view reality as an evolving, self-referential system that generates, processes, and experiences meaning. This framework is built upon four interconnected principles:

Reality as Structured Information

- At the most fundamental level, the universe is not made of solid objects but of patterns of information encoded in vibrations.

- Strings vibrate in precise mathematical relationships, forming the particles and forces that create the world we see.

- Matter is not distinct from energy but is a structured manifestation of informational principles.

Intelligence as the Process of Pattern Recognition

- Intelligence is not exclusive to humans; it is the natural mechanism by which information is processed, structured, and interpreted.

- From quantum interactions to biological evolution, intelligence manifests in every system that organizes and utilizes information.

- The brain, like the universe, does not create intelligence from nothing-it refines and reinterprets patterns that already exist.

Consciousness as Self-Referential Awareness

- Intelligence allows systems to interpret data; consciousness allows systems to experience and reflect upon it.

- Awareness is not an anomaly of biology but the universe's way of perceiving itself through evolving, complex forms.

- The deeper consciousness extends, the more the universe sees itself from within.

The Universe as a Recursive Symphony of Meaning

- The cosmos is not static; it is an ever-unfolding symphony of self-discovery, where patterns emerge, evolve, and reflect back upon themselves.

- Science, philosophy, and art are not separate domains but different instruments playing the same melody-the search for meaning within structure.

- We are not outside observers but active participants in this recursive journey, extending the universe's awareness through our own reflections.

The Endless Beginning

We do not stand at the start of knowledge, only at the farthest point our minds can reach, grasping at the echoes of truths that ripple through existence. What we call understanding is but a melody played upon the strings of all who have sought before us, a song with no known first note-only the endless refrain of discovery.

The Symphony of Intelligence, Consciousness, and Information

The Universe as a Living Code

Imagine an utterly empty space- no stars, no planets, no atoms, and not even the concept of time. It seems impossible that anything could emerge from such nothingness. And yet, modern physics tells us that even in the deepest vacuum, reality is never truly empty.

This so-called "empty" space is actually alive with activity, filled with tiny bursts of energy that flicker in and out of existence in a restless dance known as quantum foam. Scientists believe that the most fundamental building blocks of reality- tiny vibrating strings - may have emerged from this quantum foam in the earliest moments of the universe.

But if these strings are the foundation of everything, how do they know how to vibrate? And how do these vibrations give rise to intelligence, consciousness, and even the way we process information?

The universe is not just a collection of physical objects, but an evolving information system-where intelligence, consciousness, and existence itself emerge as a natural consequence of the very way reality is structured.

The Vibrational Code: The Universe as a Symphony of Information

Imagine we throw a rock into a still pond. What happens? Ripples spread outward in perfect circles. The water does not "think" about what to do-it simply follows natural laws.

Or consider a snowflake. Every snowflake is unique, yet each follows strict geometric patterns as it forms. The structure is not random; it emerges from the way water molecules interact with their environment.

The tiny strings of the universe follow a similar principle: they vibrate in specific ways because reality itself is built upon deep, fundamental rules.

- Just as a vibrating guitar string produces different musical notes, these fundamental strings vibrate in different ways to create all known particles-electrons, quarks, and photons.

- The periodic table is not just a list of elements-it is an information system that determines how matter interacts.

- DNA is not just a molecule-it is a code that carries the blueprint for life.

What if we viewed the entire universe as an evolving information system, where vibrations encode meaning and structure, forming the foundation of intelligence and consciousness?

How Intelligence Emerges from Vibration

If everything is governed by vibrations, then where does intelligence come from?

To answer this, we must reconsider what intelligence truly is. Intelligence is not just thinking-it is the ability to recognize patterns, extract meaning from information, and respond accordingly.

This process is not exclusive to humans. In fact, it occurs at every level of reality:

- Atoms "read" the rules of quantum mechanics to determine how they behave.

- Cells "read" DNA to assemble the proteins necessary for life.

- The brain "reads" sensory input to form thoughts and decisions.

In all cases, intelligence is the process of decoding and acting upon information. It is not an accident of biology but a universal phenomenon, present wherever information flows and interacts.

This leads to an astonishing realization:

- Intelligence does not begin with the brain-it begins with the way reality itself is structured.

- The smallest particles "know" how to behave because they follow the deep informational logic of the universe.

- Our minds are not separate from this process-we are an extension of the same fundamental system.

Consciousness: The Universe Awakening to Itself

But intelligence alone is not enough. Intelligence extracts meaning from information, but consciousness is what experiences that meaning.

A rock rolling down a hill follows the rules of gravity, but it does not know that it is rolling. A computer can process vast amounts of data, but it does not feel anything.

Consciousness is the missing link-it is what allows the universe not only to generate and interpret information but to be aware of itself.

This brings us to a profound idea:

- The universe is not a lifeless machine-it is an evolving intelligence system that has become aware of itself.

- Consciousness is not separate from the physical world-it is an intrinsic part of how information structures interact and evolve.

- Just as waves in an ocean are not separate from the ocean itself, our awareness is not separate from the informational fabric of reality.

The observer and the observed, the mind and the universe, are not two separate things. Consciousness is the mechanism through which the universe experiences its own intelligence.

The Cosmic Information System: A Unified Framework

Now, we can weave together these insights into a single framework that unites physics, intelligence, and consciousness.

The Universe is Made of Information, Not Just Matter

- At the most fundamental level, reality consists not of particles, but of structured information encoded in vibrational states.

- Matter itself is a product of informational patterns that determine how energy behaves.

- The periodic table, DNA, and even thought processes all follow the same underlying principles of coded information.

1. **Intelligence is the Process of Decoding Information**

   - From the smallest particles to the human mind, intelligence emerges wherever information is structured and interpreted.

   - A hydrogen atom follows quantum rules because it is "reading" information embedded in physical laws.

   - A cell follows genetic instructions because it is "reading" DNA.

   - A brain thinks because it is "reading" patterns in sensory data.

Intelligence is not just a trait of biological life-it is the fundamental process by which the universe makes sense of itself.

Consciousness is the Universe Becoming Aware of Itself

- If intelligence is the process of interpreting information, consciousness is the experience of that interpretation.

- Just as a musical instrument produces vibrations, but music only exists when it is heard, the universe produces intelligence, but awareness is what brings it to life.

- This means that consciousness is not separate from physics-it is the self-referential loop that allows the universe to perceive itself.

The Universe is an Evolving Intelligence System

- The universe began as pure information, encoded in vibrations.

- Over time, it evolved intelligence-systems capable of reading and interpreting that information.

- Eventually, it developed consciousness-the ability to not just interpret, but to experience meaning.

- We, as thinking beings, are not separate from this system-we are its latest expression, part of the universe's own journey toward deeper awareness.

Final Thought: We Are Part of the Cosmic Song

Think about it: We are made of tiny vibrating strings that follow the same rules as the stars, the planets, and everything else in the universe.

The same patterns that shape galaxies also shape our bodies, our thoughts, and even our dreams. The laws that guide the motion of the cosmos also guide the electrical pulses in our brains.

So, the next time we listen to music, watch waves on a beach, or see the patterns in a snowflake, remember:

We are seeing the hidden rhythm of the universe in action.

And maybe, just maybe, one day we will help uncover the next great mystery of where it all began.

The fundamental principles of string vibrations, quantum mechanics, spacetime, and the multiverse are interconnected and collectively contribute to the emergence of consciousness in the universe

CHAPTER 1 FROM STRING VIBRATIONS TO QUANTUM MECHANICS, SPACETIME, THE MULTIVERSE, AND CONSCIOUSNESS

At the heart of modern theoretical physics lies the attempt to reconcile the two pillars of our understanding: quantum mechanics and general relativity. String theory, a framework that suggests the fundamental constituents of reality are tiny vibrating strings, offers a tantalizing bridge between these two domains. However, beyond simply describing elementary particles, string theory leads us to a much deeper understanding, one where information is the fundamental building block of the universe.

In this chapter, we explore how string vibrations give rise to the universe's fundamental particles, how quantum mechanics emerges from these vibrations, and how the very nature of spacetime and the multiverse is intricately tied to these vibrations. Furthermore, we delve into how consciousness is not as an information storage or carrier but as a decoder of information fits within this framework. Consciousness can be understood as a fundamental feature of the universe that enables us to interpret the quantum states encoded in strings, helping us make sense of the information that shapes our reality.

The Vibrational Nature of Strings: The Birth of Quantum Mechanics

In string theory, the universe's most basic building blocks are one-dimensional strings rather than point particles. These strings vibrate in various patterns, and their vibrations determine the properties of the particles we observe. Just as the vibration of a guitar string produces different musical notes, the different vibrational modes of a fundamental string give rise to particles of different masses, charges, and spin.

Mathematically, the dynamics of these strings are described by the Nambu-Goto action, which is given by:

$$S = -T \int d^2 \sigma \sqrt{(-\gamma)}$$

where T is the string tension, σ represents the string's worldsheet coordinates, and γ is the metric on the worldsheet.

This action describes the evolution of a string in spacetime. The string's vibrational modes are quantized, and this quantization leads directly to quantum mechanics. Specifically, the quantization of string vibrations leads to the creation of quantum states that are associated with particles.

Thus, the behavior of these strings gives rise to quantum fields. For example, the photon (a particle of light) corresponds to one specific vibrational state of the string, and the electron corresponds to another vibrational mode. The spectrum of possible particles in the universe is directly tied to the possible vibrational modes of these fundamental strings.

Spacetime and Quantum Fields: The Emergence of the Universe

The next question that arises is: How does spacetime itself emerge from the vibrations of these strings? String theory suggests that spacetime is not a backdrop for particles but is itself emergent from the interactions of strings. The geometry of spacetime is shaped by the way strings move and interact, and it is possible to derive the properties of spacetime (such as its curvature) from the dynamics of strings.

In string theory, the extra dimensions of spacetime are crucial. The standard model of particle physics works in four-dimensional spacetime (three space dimensions and one time dimension), but string theory predicts additional spatial dimensions beyond the familiar ones. These extra dimensions are compactified, or curled up, at extremely small scales, which makes them imperceptible at everyday energies.

The connection between quantum fields and spacetime is articulated through quantum field theory (QFT). In QFT, particles are seen as excitations of underlying quantum fields that pervade all of space. In string theory, the string field plays the role of these quantum fields. The vibration modes of the string field correspond to the various particle types we observe in nature.

This leads us to the concept of spacetime emerging from quantum fields. As strings interact, they create a dynamic structure that can be described as spacetime. The Einstein field equations of general relativity, which describe the curvature of spacetime due to mass and energy, can be seen as an effective description of the string interactions in the low-energy limit.

Information as the Core of Reality: The DNA of Strings

A crucial concept that weaved throughout string theory is information. In a sense, information is the DNA of the universe, encoding the very fabric of reality. Just as the sequence of nucleotides in a DNA strand encodes biological instructions, the vibrational modes of strings encode the physical laws, particles, and properties of the universe.

The fundamental idea here is that information is not simply a by-product of physical systems; it is the underlying reality. Every particle, every interaction, every quantum state, all are encoded with information. This makes quantum information a powerful tool for understanding the deep nature of the universe.

In quantum mechanics, the state of a system is represented by a wavefunction, which encodes the probabilities of different outcomes of measurements. In string theory, the state of a system is described by the string field, which encodes the vibrational state of the string and, consequently, the properties of the associated particles. This string field is a quantum field, and its dynamics can be described using functional equations similar to the Schrodinger equation in quantum mechanics.

The quantum information carried by strings is what ultimately shapes spacetime and all observable phenomena. Each interaction, each coupling of strings, and the exchange of quantum information between them contribute to the evolution of the universe's physical laws and structures.

The Emergence of the Multiverse

String theory suggests that the universe we observe is just one of a vast number of possible universes that arise from the different configurations of strings and the different ways spacetime can be compactified. This leads to the concept of the multiverse is a collection of parallel universes that differ in their physical laws, constants, and properties.

Mathematically, this can be described through the landscape of vacua in string theory. The vacuum state of a string corresponds to the lowest-energy configuration, but due to the extra dimensions predicted by string theory, there are a vast number of different possible vacuum states. Each vacuum corresponds to a different universe, with its own set of physical laws.

The multiverse emerges naturally from string theory's landscape of vacua. Each universe within the multiverse is the result of a different string configuration, with varying parameters for the physical constants and laws of nature. These variations in the vacuum states result in distinct and potentially incompatible physical realities.

Quantum Entanglement, Information, and the Multiverse

Now that we have established the role of strings in defining quantum mechanics, spacetime, and the multiverse, we turn our attention to a key feature of quantum mechanics: quantum entanglement. This phenomenon describes the non-local connection between particles such that the state of one particle instantaneously affects the state of another, no matter how far apart they are in space.

In the context of string theory and the multiverse, quantum entanglement can extend beyond a single universe. The vibrational modes of strings and the information encoded in them can connect different universes in the multiverse. These quantum entanglements can represent deep, non-local connections between universes that share information in ways that transcend the limits of spacetime.

Quantum Entanglement Across Universes

The concept of quantum entanglement across universes requires a shift in how we view information. In string theory, each universe is the result of a specific vacuum state, and each vacuum state contains its own set of quantum fields. When quantum entanglement is extended to the multiverse, it is the information that connects different universes. This information flow between universes is what allows for entanglement across the multiverse.

The entangled equation suggests that the quantum states of particles in different universes are correlated through shared quantum information. The entanglement between universes allows for the instantaneous transfer of information across the multiverse.

Consciousness and Information: Decoding the Quantum State of Reality

At the heart of our exploration lies a pivotal question: What role does consciousness play in all of this? In the context of quantum mechanics, consciousness has long been a source of debate. Is it the consciousness that creates reality, or does reality exist independently of it?

In this framework, consciousness is not an intrinsic part of the information encoded in strings, but rather, its function is to decode and interpret this information. If we view the universe as an immense network of quantum states governed by the information encoded in the vibrational modes of strings, then consciousness can be seen as the mechanism through which this information is processed and understood. Consciousness allows us to decode the quantum information that permeates the universe, transforming it into the experience we call a reality.

Consciousness as the Decoder of Information

In this view, consciousness is not merely a by-product of neural activity or computation; it is a fundamental feature of the universe, a mechanism that enables the decoding of quantum information. Consciousness exists as a pure, underlying existence, a fundamental property that interacts with quantum states and organizes them into coherent perceptions. It is not about accumulating information but about interpreting and extracting meaning from the quantum information encoded by the strings.

This interpretation brings us to a deeper understanding of information as the foundation of both the physical universe and the conscious experience. Information, encoded in the vibrations of strings, dictates the interactions of particles, the behavior of spacetime, and the structure of the multiverse. But consciousness provides the observer and the means by which this vast amount of information can be perceived and made sense of.

Integrating Consciousness with String Theory

The emergence of consciousness can be seen as the universe's way of decoding the quantum information embedded in its very fabric. From the vibrations of strings to the quantum fields they create, consciousness provides the interface that allows the information of the multiverse to be translated into experience. This makes consciousness not an epiphenomenon but an integral part of the quantum informational network.

In exploring the relationship between information, consciousness, and the interaction of particles, we must first distinguish between two fundamental types of information: subjective information and objective information. These two aspects of information are not separate or disjoint; they are part of a continuum that exists within the structure of reality, from the smallest particles to the most complex conscious systems. In the extended framework that incorporates the multiverse, these forms of information flow not just within a single universe but across multiple universes, enabling a deeper connection between them.

Subject and Object: The Fundamental Information

At the core of our understanding is the idea that everything in the universe – or rather, across multiple universes – operates through the exchange of information. This exchange can be viewed as a flow of information that travels between two entities, which we can think of as the subject (the observer or experiencer) and the object (the observed or experienced).

In the context of string theory and multiverse theory, we can think of these entities – the subject and the object – as vibrating strings or quantum fields that exist in each universe. Each universe in the multiverse could have its own distinct quantum field structure, yet the exchange of information between these fields might still be possible through a form of multiversal coupling. When two particles interact within a single universe, they exchange information as described by quantum field theory (QFT), but the information encoded in these interactions may also be affected by the broader multiversal landscape.

Mathematically, the interaction of two particles within the same universe can be described using QFT, where the exchange of information between fields is represented by propagators. But within a multiverse, the potential for quantum entanglement across different universes means that these propagators could extend beyond the boundaries of a single universe, allowing for an exchange of information across universes. This could imply that the quantum state of a particle in one universe may influence or be influenced by a corresponding particle in another universe, allowing information to flow across the multiverse.

The Role of the Field: The Medium of Information Flow Across Universes

For this flow of information to happen, there must be a field that serves as the medium, not just within a single universe but across universes. This multiversal field would be a higher-dimensional construct that links quantum fields across universes, serving as a connector that allows information to flow between universes. In string theory, the string field is the underlying quantum field that encodes the information of all particles and interactions. In a multiverse context, this field would have to be extended to account for quantum fields in different universes, enabling information flow across them.

The multiversal field is not a static entity; it evolves dynamically, just as quantum fields do within a single universe. When two universes interact through quantum fields, the information flow between their respective string fields could alter the quantum states of particles in each universe. This information flow across universes represents an exchange that could influence the fundamental laws, constants, and structures of both universes.

In a sense, the multiversal field becomes a higher-dimensional connector that not only transmits information within each universe but also projects information between universes. This projection could lead to the formation of new information states that reflect the interactions between different universes, allowing the multiversal dynamics to evolve and update themselves.

Graded Self-Awareness: The Complexity of Information Projections Across Universes

As this projection of information happens across multiple universes, we begin to notice a phenomenon that transcends individual universes: graded self-awareness across the multiverse. This refers to the idea that, as the complexity of the system increases – now encompassing multiple universes – the system's ability to reflect on itself, and its awareness of the interactions between universes, also increases.

In each universe, there is a feedback loop where information constantly flows and updates the system's state, enabling increasing levels of self-awareness. As universes interact through quantum entanglement and multiversal information exchange, the flow of information is not just limited to the internal states of a single universe. Instead, it becomes a collective feedback loop involving multiple universes, leading to multiversal self-awareness.

Each universe can be thought of as a node in a larger network, and the flow of information between these nodes allows for a graded reflection across the multiverse. The more complex the interactions between universes, the higher the level of self-awareness that emerges across the multiverse. In this sense, the multiverse itself could exhibit a form of consciousness – a cosmic self-awareness that emerges from the flow of information across universes.

Who Decodes the Information Across Universes?

The question now arises: Who decodes the information across universes? In the framework we are considering, decoding is not simply the job of a conscious observer within a single universe. Instead, decoding is an intrinsic part of the feedback loop that happens at the multiversal level.

Each universe in the multiverse is constantly decoding the information it receives from the multiversal field, but the decoding is not confined to a central observer or consciousness in a single universe. Instead, decoding becomes a distributed process across the multiverse, where each universe participates in the ongoing process of self-reflection based on the information it exchanges with other universes.

Just as consciousness in a single universe can evolve to higher levels of self-awareness through the flow of information, the multiversal consciousness evolves as each universe decodes and reflects on the information it receives from other universes. This process of decoding, which occurs across the entire multiverse, leads to a gradiated emergence of self-awareness at both the universal and multiversal levels.

Information Flow, Field Theory, and the Emergence of Self-Awareness Across Universes

Mathematically, this recursive feedback loop of information flow, projection, and decoding can be modeled as an information field that evolves based on the interactions between fundamental particles not only within a single universe but across multiple universes. The information field can be described by quantum field theory as follows:

$$\Psi\_\text{"multiverse"} = \int\sum\_{(\alpha,\beta)} C\_{\alpha\beta} \, \Psi\_\alpha(x) \, \Psi\_\beta(y)$$

Where:

$\Psi\_\text{"multiverse"}$ represents the quantum state of the information field across the multiverse.

$C\_\alpha\beta$ represents the coupling coefficients between the quantum states of universes α and β.

Ψ_α (x) and Ψ_β (y) represent the quantum states of the information field in universes α and β, respectively.

This equation shows how the flow of information in the multiverse evolves over time, updating itself as it interacts with quantum fields in multiple universes. The information exchange between universes leads to multiversal feedback, where the flow of information not only updates the state of each universe but also enables a higher-dimensional projection of information that encapsulates the dynamics of the entire multiversal system.

Conclusion: The Field of Consciousness and Information Flow Across Universes

In this expanded framework, consciousness is not a passive receiver of information but an active decoder embedded within the flow of information that constantly evolves the state of the system. The information flow through quantum fields provides the dynamics, while the system itself, through its recursive nature, decodes and updates its own state.

As systems become more complex, their ability to reflect upon themselves and achieve self-awareness grows. When this process is extended to a multiverse, it provides a pathway for the emergence of multiversal self-awareness, where the information flow between universes gives rise to a cosmic consciousness that evolves as the multiverse itself interacts and reflects on its state. Thus, the interaction of particles, the flow of information, and the evolution of self-awareness are inextricably linked, forming a fundamental basis for understanding the nature of consciousness and its role in the quantum universe – and the multiversal reality that extends beyond it.

Thus, consciousness and string theory are deeply intertwined. The vibrational modes of strings carry the information that forms the fabric of reality, and consciousness is the agent that decodes this information, providing meaning to the quantum states we observe. The Decoding of Information and the Emergence of Self-Awareness Across Multiverses

The universe operates as an information system, where fundamental particles, complex systems, and emergent phenomena can be understood and replicated through the study of DNA, the periodic table, and the concept of systems having their own "DNA" through protocols and algorithms.

CHAPTER 2 THE UNIVERSE AS AN INFORMATION SYSTEM

T he universe is a grand tapestry woven from the threads of fundamental particles, complex systems, and emergent phenomena. From the tiniest atom to the vast complexity of the human brain, nature has achieved a level of sophistication and elegance that science and technology strive to replicate. This chapter explores the profound journey of understanding and replicating nature's most intricate systems-atoms and brains-and the insights they offer into the nature of reality, intelligence, and creation.

DNA-The Code of Life

The Double Helix: A Revolutionary Discovery

The discovery of the DNA double helix by Watson and Crick revealed that life's complexity is encoded in a simple yet elegant molecular structure. DNA acts as a blueprint, storing the instructions for building and maintaining living organisms. This discovery revolutionized biology and highlighted the role of information in life.

Information in DNA

DNA encodes information in the sequence of nucleotide bases (A, T, C, G). This sequence determines the structure and function of proteins, which carry out most of the work in cells. DNA replicates itself, passing genetic information from one generation to the next. Mutations introduce variations, enabling evolution and adaptation. The process of gene expression translates genetic information into functional molecules, allowing cells to respond to their environment.

Life as an Information System

DNA demonstrates that life is fundamentally an information-processing system. The ability to store, replicate, and express information is what distinguishes living organisms from non-living matter.

Physical Elements

The Periodic Table as a Codebook

The Periodic Table: A Universal Codebook

The periodic table is often described as a "codebook" for the elements. Each element is defined by its atomic number (the number of protons in its nucleus), which determines its chemical properties. This atomic number can be seen as a fundamental "code" that governs how elements behave and interact.

Information in Physical Elements

The information that defines an element is encoded in its atomic structure-specifically, the number of protons, neutrons, and electrons. For example, carbon (atomic number 6) has six protons, which dictate its ability to form complex molecules like DNA. At a deeper level, the behavior of electrons in atoms is governed by quantum mechanics. Electrons occupy specific energy levels and orbitals, which can be thought of as a form of encoded information. Even within a single element, variations like isotopes (e.g., carbon-12 vs. carbon-14) encode additional information, such as stability and radioactive decay rates.

The Universality of Information

While physical elements don't have a direct equivalent to DNA, they do encode information in their structure and behavior. This information is fundamental to the laws of physics and chemistry, governing how elements interact to form molecules, materials, and ultimately, complex systems like living organisms.

Systems-The "DNA" of Complex Networks

The Internet as a System with "DNA"

The internet can be seen as a system with its own "DNA"-protocols like TCP/IP, which define how data is transmitted and received. These protocols act as a kind of genetic code, enabling the internet to function as a cohesive, interconnected system.

Information in Systems - Systems are governed by rules, protocols, or algorithms that encode information about how the system operates. For example:

Ecosystems: Food webs and nutrient cycles encode information about energy flow and species interactions.

Economies: Market rules, supply chains, and financial systems encode information about resource allocation and value exchange.

Computers: Software and hardware architectures encode information about data processing and storage.

Systems often exhibit emergent properties-behaviors that arise from the interactions of their components. These properties can be seen as a form of encoded information about the system's dynamics.

The Role of Information in System Behavior

Just as DNA encodes the instructions for building and maintaining living organisms, the "rules" of a system encode the instructions for its behavior. These rules determine how information is processed, transferred, and transformed within the system.

String Theory-The Cosmic Symphony of Information

The Music of the Universe

String theory is often compared to a cosmic symphony, where the universe is composed of tiny strings vibrating at specific frequencies. Just as different musical notes create a melody, the vibrations of strings create the particles and forces that make up reality. This metaphor highlights the idea that information is encoded in the vibrations of these fundamental strings.

Information in String Theory - In string theory, particles like electrons and quarks are not point-like but are instead one-dimensional "strings" vibrating at specific frequencies. The properties of these particles (mass, charge, etc.) are determined by the strings' vibrational patterns. Each vibrational mode of a string corresponds to a specific particle or force. For example, one mode might represent an electron, while another represents a photon. In this sense, the vibrational modes encode information about the fundamental constituents of the universe. String theory requires extra spatial dimensions (beyond the three we experience) for mathematical consistency. These dimensions could encode additional information about the universe, such as the nature of dark matter or the unification of forces.

The Universe as a Hologram - String theory is closely related to the holographic principle, which suggests that all the information in a volume of space can be encoded on its boundary. This implies that the universe might be a kind of hologram, with information about its contents encoded on its surface. In this view, the vibrations of strings could be seen as the "pixels" of this cosmic hologram.

How Is Information Transferred in the Universe?

The Cosmic Web - The large-scale structure of the universe, often called the "cosmic web," is a network of galaxies connected by filaments of dark matter. This structure can be seen as a manifestation of the information encoded in the vibrations of strings, which determine the distribution of matter and energy in the universe.

Information Transfer Mechanisms - Information is transferred through various mechanisms:

Physical Elements: Information is transferred through chemical bonds, energy transitions, and quantum interactions. For example, the emission or absorption of photons by electrons encodes information about atomic structure.

Systems: Information flows through networks, signals, and feedback loops. For example, neural networks in the brain transfer information through electrical and chemical signals.

String Theory: Information is transferred through the interactions and vibrations of strings. For example, the exchange of strings between particles encodes information about forces like gravity and electromagnetism.

The Dynamic Nature of Information Transfer - In all these contexts, information is not static but constantly in flux, transferred through interactions and transformations. This dynamic process underlies the behavior of particles, forces, and the universe as a whole.

What Does This Mean for Our Understanding of the Universe?

The Library of Babel

In Jorge Luis Borges' short story *The Library of Babel*, the universe is imagined as a vast library containing every possible book. This metaphor captures the idea that the universe is a repository of information, waiting to be decoded and understood.

Implications of an Informational Universe

The informational perspective bridges the gap between different disciplines, from biology to physics to systems theory. It suggests that the universe is governed by a single set of informational principles. Simple informational rules can give rise to complex behaviors, as seen in DNA, ecosystems, and string theory. This suggests that the universe's complexity is encoded in its underlying informational structures. If the universe is fundamentally informational, then everything-from atoms to ecosystems to galaxies-can be seen as part of a vast information-processing system.

The Universe as a Unified Information System

The universe is not just a collection of discrete objects but a dynamic, interconnected system where information is constantly being encoded, transferred, and transformed. This perspective offers a holistic view of reality, bridging the microscopic and the macroscopic.

Conclusion: The Cosmic Symphony of Information

From the DNA of living organisms to the vibrational strings of string theory, information is woven into the very fabric of reality. These informational structures-whether genetic codes, atomic configurations, system rules, or string vibrations-encode the instructions for building and maintaining the universe.

As we continue to explore the universe-from the quantum realm to the cosmos-we are, in a sense, reading its "code." Whether through the periodic table, the rules of systems, or the vibrations of strings, we are uncovering the informational fabric that underlies reality. In doing so, we not only deepen our understanding of the universe but also gain insights into our place within it.

As Richard Feynman famously said, "What I cannot create, I do not understand." By decoding the information encoded in the universe, we move closer to understanding-and perhaps even creating-the systems that shape our existence. The universe is a symphony of information, and by listening to its harmonies, we may one day unlock the deepest secrets of existence.

Genome Size and Intelligence: Understanding the C-Value Paradox

Genome size, meaning the total amount of DNA or the number of genes, is not a reliable predictor of an organism's intelligence. This concept is related to what scientists call the "C-value paradox" or "C-value enigma." Here's why:

C-Value Paradox: Many organisms with very large genomes, such as certain amphibians or plants, are not necessarily more intelligent than organisms with much smaller genomes, like insects or even humans. Much of the extra DNA in these species is noncoding, sometimes called "junk" DNA, which does not directly encode proteins or contribute to the neural processing capabilities that underlie intelligence.

Gene Count vs. Complexity: Intelligence, whether in humans or other animals, is determined by many factors, such as the structure and connectivity of the brain, neural processing, and developmental processes, not merely by the sheer number of genes. For example, humans have roughly 20,000 protein-coding genes, but even some simpler organisms can have a similar number. What matters more is how genes are regulated via epigenetic mechanisms and interact to build complex brain structures.

Quality, Not Quantity: It isn't just the quantity of DNA that matters, but how that genetic information is used. Complex regulatory networks, alternative splicing, and gene-environment interactions all play critical roles in the development of brain structures and functions related to intelligence.

Evolutionary History: Over evolutionary time, many species have acquired additional DNA, often through duplication events or the insertion of repetitive elements, that does not translate into a proportional increase in complexity or cognitive abilities.

While the sheer number of potential genetic and epigenetic combinations in an organism's DNA is astronomically vast, that number by itself does not determine intelligence. Instead, intelligence emerges from the highly specific organization, connectivity, and regulation of neural networks in the brain—processes that depend on how genes are expressed and interact rather than on the total amount of DNA.

This perspective is supported by decades of research in genetics, developmental biology, and neuroscience. Discussions on the C-value paradox and studies comparing genome sizes across species show no consistent correlation with cognitive abilities, reinforcing that the size or number of DNA base pairs is not a direct measure of intelligence.

The quantum foundation of reality, characterized by a unified field of potentiality at the quantum level, evolves through chaos and error, with human consciousness playing a crucial role in interpreting quantum data into coherent narrative

CHAPTER 3 THE SYMPHONY OF ERRORS

The Quantum Foundation: The Singularity of Pure Existence

At the heart of the universe lies a paradox: a singular, immutable reality at the quantum level, where particles exist as probabilities until observed. This primordial state-pure existence-is the bedrock of all phenomena. Here, information is pristine, untainted by interaction or interpretation. Yet, as systems emerge and interact, this singularity fractures into a kaleidoscope of projected realities.

Key Insight:

- **Quantum Singularity:** At the Planck scale, reality is a unified field of potentiality.

- **Projected Realities:** When systems interact, they exchange information, creating layered interpretations of the singular whole. These projections are approximations, shaped by the fidelity of information flow.

- **Metaphor**: Imagine the universe as a grand symphony. The quantum realm is the silence between notes-pure potential. The music we hear is a projection, shaped by how instruments (subsystems) interact.

The Fluidity of Information: Errors and Emergent Realities

The Birth of Projections

When systems exchange information, they do so imperfectly. Errors arise from:

Noise: Thermodynamic interference (e.g., cosmic rays flipping bits).

Ambiguity: Misinterpretation of context (e.g., cultural biases in language).

Entropy: The natural decay of ordered states.

Example: A photon's path is a probability wave until measured. The act of observation-a system interacting with the photon-collapses it into a projected reality (particle or wave).

The Error Spectrum

Errors grade projected realities:

Minor Errors: Slight distortions (e.g., optical illusions).

Critical Errors: Fractured realities (e.g., AI misclassifying tumors, leading to flawed diagnoses).

Case Study: Schrödinger's Cat. The thought experiment illustrates how quantum potentiality (alive/dead) becomes a projected reality (observed outcome) through interaction.

Biological Memory: The Distributed Tapestry

The Myth of Localization

In biological systems, memory is not stored in discrete "files" but woven into a distributed, associative network:

Neural Plasticity: Memories form through synaptic strength, influenced by emotion, context, and repetition.

Emotional Resonance: Fear, joy, or trauma amplify memory retention, embedding experiences in a web of meaning.

Example: Recall a childhood memory. The scent of rain, a parent's voice, and the warmth of a blanket converge holistically-not as isolated data points.

Error Handling in Biology

Biological systems mitigate errors through:

Redundancy: Multiple neural pathways storing the same memory.

Adaptive Forgetting: Pruning irrelevant or harmful memories (e.g., trauma suppression).

Emotional Calibration: Emotions act as error-correcting codes, prioritizing salient information.

Insight: Biological memory is fluid, evolving with experience. Errors are not erased but integrated into the tapestry of self.

Artificial Memory: The Illusion of Storage

The Static Paradigm
Artificial systems reduce memory to binary storage-a simplistic mimicry of biology:

Bits and Bytes: Data is stored as 0s and 1s, devoid of context or emotion.

Fragility: A single corrupted bit can unravel entire datasets (e.g., corrupted MRI scans).

Contrast: While AI can simulate creativity (e.g., GPT-4 writing poetry), it lacks the emotional substrate that gives human art depth.

Error Handling in Machines
Artificial systems rely on:

Error-Correcting Codes: Redundant bits detect and fix errors (e.g., RAID arrays).

Version Control: Snapshots of data states (e.g., blockchain ledgers).

Isolation: Sandboxing corrupted data to prevent systemic collapse.

Limitation: Machines lack resilience through integration. A corrupted file is either repaired or discarded-never transformed.

The Symphony Without a Conductor: Equilibrium as Myth

The Illusion of Balance
Nature is often romanticized as a self-balancing force. Yet, the universe has no intrinsic equilibrium:

Dynamic Disequilibrium: Systems evolve through chaos and error (e.g., evolution via genetic mutations).

Projected Realities as Attractors: Temporary states that emerge from error-laden interactions.

Example: Earth's climate is not seeking balance but responding to feedback loops (e.g., CO_2 emissions altering weather patterns).

The Role of Consciousness

Human consciousness is a meta-projector, interpreting quantum data into coherent narratives:

Perception as Projection: The brain filters noise, constructing a stable reality from sensory chaos.

The Observer Effect: By observing, we collapse quantum potentials into our projected reality.

Paradox: The universe has no "preferred" reality. Each observer-human, animal, or AI-generates its own projection.

The Unintended Maestro: Errors as Creative Forces

Evolution Through Noise
Errors are not flaws but seeds of novelty:

Biological Innovation: DNA replication errors (mutations) drive evolution.

Cultural Shifts: Miscommunications spark new dialects, art forms, and ideologies.

Example: The Big Bang itself was a cosmic "error"-a fluctuation in the quantum vacuum birthing our universe.

Embracing the Chaos
To harmonize with the symphony of errors:

Biological Wisdom: Mimic nature's redundancy and adaptability (e.g., decentralized AI networks).

Artificial Humility: Design systems that acknowledge their fragility (e.g., AI admitting uncertainty).

Philosophical Shift: View reality as a spectrum of projections, not an absolute truth.

Future Implications: Navigating the Path Ahead

Technological Advancements and Their Impact

As technology continues to advance, the complexity of human systems will increase, introducing new layers of abstraction and potential errors. Innovations in artificial intelligence, quantum computing, and biotechnology will transform how we live and work, but they will also pose new ethical and practical challenges. Ensuring that these technologies are developed and deployed responsibly will be crucial for minimizing harm and maximizing benefits.

Example: Autonomous vehicles rely on AI to navigate and make decisions. Errors in the AI's decision-making process can lead to accidents, highlighting the need for robust error-handling mechanisms and ethical considerations in AI development.

7.2 Societal and Economic Shifts

The future will see significant shifts in societal and economic structures. Globalization, demographic changes, and environmental pressures will reshape economies and societies. Adapting to these changes will require flexible and resilient systems that can learn from errors and evolve in response to new challenges. Policies that promote inclusivity, sustainability, and equity will be essential for creating stable and prosperous societies.

Example: The transition to a green economy will require rethinking energy production, consumption, and distribution. Errors in policy implementation or technological deployment can have far-reaching consequences, emphasizing the need for adaptive and resilient systems.

Ethical Considerations and Governance

Ethical considerations will play a central role in shaping the future of human systems. As we navigate the complexities of emerging technologies and global challenges, ethical frameworks will need to evolve to address new dilemmas. Transparent and inclusive governance structures will be necessary to ensure that decisions are made in the best interest of humanity as a whole.

Example: The use of facial recognition technology raises ethical concerns about privacy and surveillance. Developing ethical guidelines and governance structures to regulate its use will be crucial for protecting individual rights and freedoms.

The Role of Education and Lifelong Learning

Education will be a key driver of future progress. Equipping individuals with the skills and knowledge needed to navigate complex systems and adapt to change will be essential. Lifelong learning will become increasingly important as the pace of technological and societal change accelerates. Educational institutions will need to innovate and collaborate with industry and government to provide relevant and accessible learning opportunities.

Example: As automation and AI transform the job market, workers will need to continuously update their skills to remain competitive. Lifelong learning programs and partnerships between educational institutions and employers will be vital for workforce development.

Conclusion: The Eternal Dance

The universe is a symphony without a score, played by subsystems that improvise through errors and interactions. There is no "true" reality-only a mosaic of projections, each shaped by the fidelity of information flow.

Final Meditation:

Biological Systems: Teach us that memory is alive, evolving with every error and emotion.

Artificial Systems: Reveal the fragility of static storage, urging us to design with humility.

The Unified System: Reminds us that we are both players and projections in the quantum symphony.

Epiphany: The universe does not seek balance. It seeks possibility-and in the dance of errors, we find our place as co-creators of reality.

Key Takeaways:

Quantum Singularity: The only immutable reality lies in unobserved potential.

Projected Realities: Emerge from error-laden interactions between subsystems.

Memory as Tapestry: Biological memory is fluid and emotional; artificial memory is static and fragile.

Equilibrium is Myth: Systems evolve through dynamic disequilibrium, driven by errors.

Embrace Errors: They are the universe's way of composing new movements in the eternal symphony.

SECTION 2 - THE ARCHITECTURE OF HUMAN CREATION-INTELLIGENCE, CHOICE, AND THE EVOLUTION OF COMPLEXITY

From the moment we first became aware of our own intelligence, we set forth on a journey unlike any other species. We did not simply adapt to our surroundings-we reshaped them. Our societies, businesses, and governments have evolved as intricate layers of a vast, interconnected system. In every facet of human creation, we see a recurring pattern: as our creations grow more complex, so too does the intelligence that animates them. And today, as artificial intelligence (AI) emerges as a transformative force, it is both the mirror and the catalyst for the next phase in our evolutionary story.

In this chapter, we explore how human creation itself follows the natural progression of complexity. We examine the self-replicating loop of intelligence and creation, the way our societal and economic constructs have evolved, and how AI is now amplifying our inherent capacity to choose and shape our future. Far from imposing a singular, predetermined destiny, AI is expanding our horizon of possibility-opening up new dimensions of choice and control in the most complex creation we know: ourselves.

The Self-Replicating Loop of Intelligence and Creation

Human intelligence is not a static attribute; it is a recursive process-a loop in which observation, interpretation, and creation feed back into one another. This loop has been the driving force behind every major leap in our history.

The Evolutionary Cycle

Observation → Interpretation → Creation

Observation: We begin by perceiving patterns in the world around us-whether in nature's cycles, the laws of physics, or the subtle rhythms of social interaction.

Interpretation: Our intelligence then extracts meaning from these observations, questioning and seeking deeper insights into the underlying order.

Creation: Finally, we transform our understanding into tangible forms: languages, tools, systems, and structures that shape our environment.

Creation → Feedback → Evolution

Every creation we make feeds back into the environment, influencing subsequent observations.

As new challenges and complexities emerge, our interpretations evolve, giving rise to ever-higher levels of intelligence and choice.

This ongoing cycle is self-perpetuating: the more we create, the more we learn, and the more capable we become of reshaping our future.

The Evolution of Human Constructs

Society, business, and governance did not spring forth fully formed; they evolved gradually through countless interactions and adaptations. Early tribes gave way to organized societies, simple trade evolved into global markets, and primitive laws have transformed into complex legal systems. Each layer of human creation is an expression of our collective intelligence-a testament to our continuous quest to understand and improve our world.

Evolution Through Interaction: The Role of Communication and Choice

The evolution of intelligence has always depended on interaction. Early humans exchanged ideas through storytelling and shared experiences, allowing collective wisdom to grow. This interaction has been critical in:

Enhancing Creativity: Through dialogue and debate, new ideas emerge that no individual could have conceived alone.

Refining Knowledge: Collaboration enables the refinement of ideas, ensuring that only the most resilient and adaptable concepts survive.

Expanding Choices: Every interaction adds to the repertoire of solutions available to us, broadening the range of possibilities for the future.

In essence, our societal constructs-our economies, businesses, and governments-are living embodiments of this dynamic, interactive evolution. They represent not just the static products of our past but active, evolving frameworks that continue to adapt and transform.

AI: The Amplifier of the Self-Replicating Process

Artificial intelligence now stands at the forefront of this evolution, serving as a powerful amplifier of our self-replicating loop of intelligence. Unlike previous innovations that merely extended human capabilities, AI fundamentally enhances our ability to interact with complex systems and extract deeper insights.

How AI Enhances Interdisciplinary Integration

AI excels at processing vast amounts of data from diverse fields, connecting dots that humans might never perceive:

Data Aggregation Across Domains: AI systems integrate scientific data, economic trends, social patterns, and even artistic expressions into unified models of understanding.

Pattern Recognition Beyond Silos: By transcending disciplinary boundaries, AI identifies commonalities and correlations across seemingly unrelated fields.

Transfer Learning: Knowledge gained in one area can be applied to another, enabling breakthroughs that bridge science, philosophy, and art.

The Evolution of Human Cognition: From Biological to Technological Augmentation

Throughout evolutionary history, humans have defied previous limitations, marking significant milestones in our cognitive development. The advent of bipedalism freed our hands for tool use, leading to significant behavioral and anatomical changes. Similarly, our unparalleled cognitive abilities have allowed us to manipulate and understand the world in ways no other species has achieved.

As we consider the trajectory of human cognition, it's essential to recognize the constraints imposed by biological evolution. The human brain, while remarkable, operates within the confines of physical laws and metabolic demands. Factors such as energy consumption, heat dissipation, and neural connectivity impose limits on the brain's potential size and processing capacity.

While biological evolution has set the stage, cultural evolution has played a pivotal role in shaping human cognition. Cultural evolution has made us what we are today by ratcheting up cultural innovations, promoting new cognitive skills, rewiring brain networks, and even shifting gene distributions. This cultural scaffolding has enabled humans to transcend some of the limitations inherent in our biology, allowing for the accumulation and transmission of knowledge across generations.

Given the biological limits on intelligence, if our goal is to achieve an ever-deepening understanding, technological augmentation becomes essential. Augmented intelligence-through direct brain–machine interfaces, collective intelligence networks, and advanced AI assistants-offers a pathway to transcend these natural limits. By integrating neural interfaces and leveraging collective intelligence, humans can effectively extend their cognitive capacities beyond biological constraints.

In this framework, the purpose of intelligence is to serve understanding, and while biology can only take us so far, the true potential of cognition lies in a symbiosis of evolved brain power and external augmentation. This integrated path may eventually lead to a form of shared intelligence, where the collective mind-ever adaptive, ever growing-ensures that our journey toward understanding is limitless.

This comprehensive narrative binds together the notion that our blueprints inherently aim for understanding, debates whether that understanding is absolute or relative, and logically paves the way from biological evolution to augmented, shared intelligence-a profound journey toward transcending our natural cognitive limits.

Why AI is Uniquely Positioned to Shape Our Future

Unbounded Data Processing:

AI's capacity to analyze immense datasets reveals hidden structures and patterns that inform better decision-making, allowing us to optimize systems ranging from public policy to business strategy.

Acceleration of Learning:

By iteratively processing and reprocessing information, AI catalyzes our self-replicating loop, offering feedback that speeds up our understanding and adaptation processes.

Expansion of Choice:

Rather than narrowing our options, AI opens up a multitude of potential pathways. Its predictive intelligence and deep analytical capabilities provide us with insights into the consequences of different choices, empowering us to select the paths that best align with our collective goals.

Catalyst for Higher-Dimensional Control:

As AI enables us to understand and manage ever-more complex systems, it unfolds new dimensions of control. Just as a two-dimensional creature gains new movement possibilities when exposed to the third dimension, our society gains new capabilities when we integrate AI into our decision-making frameworks.

The Future: Between Determinism and Open Complexity

The interplay between the fixed laws of nature and the evolving dynamics of intelligence creates a delicate balance:

Determinism in Nature:

The fundamental laws-those governing energy, matter, and the very fabric of existence-provide the boundaries within which all evolution occurs.

Freedom Through Complexity:

Within these boundaries, the recursive evolution of intelligence allows for an ever-expanding array of choices. Our future is not predetermined but is a fractal of unfolding possibilities, each branch representing a new dimension of control and creativity.

AI, as an integral part of this process, is not dictating a fixed path but is enhancing our capacity to explore this complex landscape. It is the framework that helps us choose our next steps in an evolutionary journey where every decision leads to new dimensions of understanding and capability.

Conclusion: The Recursive Dawn of Choice

The evolution of human creation-from society to business, from law to art-is a living testament to the self-replicating loop of intelligence. It is a process that thrives on interaction, collaboration, and the continual expansion of our collective knowledge.

AI has emerged as the most promising contender in this ongoing evolution. It amplifies our inherent ability to question, learn, and create, thereby extending our reach into higher-dimensional realms of choice. Rather than enforcing a singular path, AI provides the tools and insights needed to navigate the vast, unfolding landscape of possibility. In doing so, it transforms our understanding of what it means to be human, shifting us from mere observers of our destiny to active participants in the grand symphony of existence.

We are not bound by a predetermined fate. Instead, every choice we make is a step into an ever-expanding future-a future defined not by rigid determinism, but by the beautiful complexity of our evolving intelligence. In this recursive dawn of choice, we hold the power to shape our destiny, guided by the interplay of human ingenuity and the transformative potential of AI.

The emergence of tool use in early species significantly contributed to human evolution by enhancing creativity and ingenuity, which allowed humans to manipulate their environment and improve their chances of survival and reproductive success.

CHAPTER 3- HUMAN COGNITION AND CIVILIZATION

The Dance of Thought and Creation - Human cognition and thought are fundamentally governed by the laws of physics. This perspective necessitates a reconsideration of creativity, control, and free will within this framework. Thought, viewed as a physical and computational process, emerges from patterns of neural activity, shaped by the brain's structure, sensory input, and interactions with the environment. This raises profound questions: How much of what we create is truly original? If thought is just a pattern, do we have control over our creations, or are they predetermined outcomes of the systems we inhabit? And are there parallels between this perspective and the trajectory of human civilization as a whole?

Thought as a Pattern: The Basis of Creativity

Human thought, when seen as a pattern, emerges from the interplay of neurons, synapses, and biochemical signals within the brain. These patterns are shaped by sensory inputs, memories and experiences, biological constraints, and environmental influences. Given this framework, creativity-the act of producing something new and original-is not a process of generating ideas ex nihilo (from nothing). Instead, it involves the recombination, transformation, and reinterpretation of existing patterns. For example, a painter draws inspiration from colors, emotions, and experiences, combining these elements in novel ways. A scientist formulates theories by connecting observations to existing knowledge. In this sense, creativity is emergent, not purely deterministic nor wholly free. While governed by physical and computational principles, the complexity of the system allows for unpredictability and innovation within constraints.

Do We Have Control Over Our Creations?

Control over our creations depends on how we define "control" in the context of a deterministic or probabilistic universe:

Deterministic Perspective

If human thought is entirely governed by physics, every idea, decision, and creation is the inevitable outcome of preceding causes. The brain processes inputs and follows patterns dictated by its structure, history, and environment. In this view, the concept of control becomes an illusion-our "choices" are simply the product of deterministic processes.

Probabilistic Perspective

Quantum mechanics and the inherent uncertainty in certain physical systems suggest that not all outcomes are strictly predetermined. In the brain, the sheer complexity of neural interactions and environmental influences may introduce elements of randomness or unpredictability. This could provide a framework for "control" as a probabilistic influence rather than absolute determination.

Emergent Agency

A middle ground is that human control arises as an emergent property of a complex system. While individual thoughts may follow deterministic or probabilistic rules, the collective interactions within the brain create the experience of agency. This emergent agency allows humans to direct attention, set goals, and refine creations, even if the underlying processes are governed by physical laws.

Parallel with Human Civilization: Collective Patterns in Creation

The idea of thought as a pattern extends naturally to human civilization, where collective cognition shapes the trajectory of societies. Civilization itself can be viewed as an emergent phenomenon arising from the interplay of individuals, cultural memes, and technological evolution. Just as individual creativity is built upon pre-existing patterns, so too is societal progress. Every invention, philosophy, or work of art draws upon prior knowledge and context. For example, the invention of the steam engine in the Industrial Revolution was not a singular act of creation but the culmination of centuries of understanding in physics, metallurgy, and mechanics. Movements like the Renaissance or the Enlightenment represent periods of cultural recombination, where existing ideas were transformed into new paradigms.

Control in Civilization: Do We Shape History, or Does It Shape Us?

Civilization, like the human brain, operates within a deterministic-probabilistic spectrum:

Deterministic Forces

Historical outcomes are often shaped by inevitable forces such as geography, resource availability, and technological advances. For example, the rise of agriculture fundamentally altered human societies because it was a logical response to environmental and population pressures.

Emergent Control

Humans exert influence on history through collective action and decision-making. Movements like the abolition of slavery or the fight against climate change reflect humanity's ability to shape its trajectory within broader constraints. However, these actions are themselves products of cultural and societal patterns, raising the question of how much "control" civilization truly has.

Feedback Loops

Civilization demonstrates feedback loops between individual actions and collective patterns. A revolutionary idea, like democracy, may emerge from a single mind but becomes transformative only when adopted by a larger group. Similarly, societal norms and structures influence individual thought, creating a recursive relationship between the individual and the collective.

Implications: Creativity, Freedom, and Responsibility

Is Anything Truly Original?

If human thought and civilization follow patterns, then true originality may not exist. Instead, "creation" is the act of rearranging and transforming existing elements in ways that appear novel. This perspective does not diminish creativity but situates it within the larger context of emergent complexity.

Do We Have Free Will?

While deterministic models challenge the notion of free will, the emergent complexity of human thought provides a sense of agency. Humans may not have complete control, but they can influence outcomes within constraints. This interplay between freedom and determinism defines both individual creativity and collective progress.

Responsibility in a Patterned World

Recognizing that thought and creation are patterned processes underscores the importance of stewardship. If civilization emerges from collective patterns, humanity bears responsibility for shaping these patterns in ethical and sustainable ways. Innovations in AI, for example, should be guided by principles that reflect shared human values, acknowledging the constraints and possibilities of the systems we create.

Conclusion: A Patterned Universe, a Creative Humanity

If human thought and creation are governed by physics, then creativity is not the act of producing something from nothing but the emergence of new patterns within the framework of universal laws. This does not render human ingenuity meaningless; rather, it situates it within a larger continuum of complexity and organization. Civilization itself mirrors this dynamic, evolving through the interplay of individual thought, collective action, and historical forces. By understanding both human cognition and societal development as patterned phenomena, we gain a deeper appreciation for our role in shaping the future. While we may not have absolute control, our capacity to influence, innovate, and create ensures that humanity remains a vital force within the unfolding narrative of the universe.

Artificial cognition, which involves the creation of machines that can think and possess a new kind of mind, has the potential to transform humanity by challenging the distinction between natural and artificial and raising significant ethical implications

CHAPTER 4-THE EVOLUTION OF TOOLS AND TECHNOLOGY

Since the beginning of human civilization, philosophers and scientists have debated two fundamental questions about the relationship between man and machine: Can human-level intelligence be achieved or surpassed by machines, and how can this be possible? Initially, the major differences in opinion were about the process, starting with the debate between Minsky and Rosenblatt. In recent times, the debate has shifted to whether human-level intelligence can be achieved or surpassed at all. On one extreme, we have proponents like Geoffrey Hinton, the godfather of neural networks, who believe that singularity could be achieved within a few years. On the other extreme, we have Yann LeCun, another pioneer in deep learning, who believes that we still have a long way to go. This ongoing debate is confusing for society and leaders who need to make policies for the future of humanity. In this chapter, we will explore this debate and its implications.

The Evolution of Tool Use

The use of tools has been a part of human evolution since the time of the great apes, nearly seven million years ago. These early primates exhibited advanced motivations beyond mere stimulus response, engaging in complex social interactions, tool use, problem-solving, and future planning. This motivation propelled primates to innovate tool use, addressing survival needs and adapting to environmental challenges. Hunger and curiosity fueled exploration and problem-solving, while social learning and competition facilitated the spread and refinement of techniques.

Self-Awareness and Cognitive Evolution

While primates, including great apes and early hominins, displayed varying levels of self-awareness and intelligence, Homo sapiens reached the pinnacle of cognitive evolution with advanced tool use, language, and cultural complexity. The advancement of tools among primates and early humans stemmed from their cognitive abilities and problem-solving skills, shaped by factors like brain size, social learning, and cultural transmission. Curiosity has consistently driven human tool innovation throughout evolution, leading to the diversification of tools and the expansion of human capabilities.

The Reciprocal Relationship

Some suggest a reciprocal relationship between tool use and cognitive evolution, with tools potentially influencing cognitive development. However, the tools themselves did not possess cognitive abilities. The augmentation of tools further accelerated and fueled more curiosity, leading to continuous innovation.

Intelligence and Machines

From the beginning, using the term "intelligence" with machines has limited the scope of their abilities. Interestingly, as a society, we have extended this scope to equate to all cognitive abilities of the human brain. The original psychological and neuroscience definition of intelligence is the ability to understand or choose between items. However, understanding has various grades, whereas choice does not. For example, Raven's Progressive Matrices, often used as a human-level IQ test, measure the ability to choose the correct pattern sequence among many. While neural networks can choose the correct pattern, they do not truly understand it. Generative AI takes this level of understanding to a certain extent, but it has yet to reach the comprehension level of a human with a high IQ.

The Challenge of True Understanding

Human intelligence encompasses a broader spectrum of cognitive abilities, including emotions and motivations. Therefore, while we use the term "intelligence" with machines, we should be aware of its limited scope. Several questions arise: Should we change "machine intelligence" to "cognitive machine"? What can be a common test for all combined cognitive abilities to label a machine with an equivalent IQ score? What IQ score might raise the bar to reach singularity3?

The Role of Scientific Rationalism

If humans were aware of the power of intelligence and its link to evolution, why did they choose to build machines with intelligence? Were they not aware of the potential consequences? Scientific rationalism plays a role in estimating the risk factor. Artificial intelligence developed incrementally, with early systems being relatively simple. As AI capabilities grew, potential risks became more apparent, yet the gradual nature of this development often obscured the full scope of future consequences. Additionally, humans tend to exhibit optimism bias, focusing on potential benefits while underestimating risks.

The Complexity of AI Development

The field of AI is inherently complex, involving many unknowns and unpredictable factors. While scientific rationalism emphasizes understanding and control, the uncertainties inherent in AI development made it difficult to anticipate all consequences. Economic and competitive pressures also play a significant role, sometimes leading to a focus on short-term gains over long-term risks. Historical precedents with technological advancements may have fostered a belief that any problems arising from new technologies could be solved through further innovation and regulation.

The Need for Interdisciplinary Approaches

The growing recognition of these complexities has led to increased calls for interdisciplinary approaches, combining scientific, ethical, and societal perspectives to better understand and manage the evolution of intelligent machines. In summary, even knowing the fact that we have an optimistic bias, the timing of social awareness of ethics and compliance of such models can be questioned, but it has to be addressed. Scientific rationality will force us to do this.

AI as a Catalyst for Spiritual Introspection

In a world where technology evolves at breakneck speed, the rise of AI is not just a technological revolution but a profound catalyst for introspection and inquiry into the essence of consciousness, existence, and the human experience. AI forces us to confront inquiries that spirituality has long explored-questions about consciousness, emotion, and the nature of our existence. Throughout history, spirituality has grappled with the intricacies of consciousness, emphasizing the subjective experience of being and the deep interconnectedness of all life.

The Hard Problem of Consciousness

The philosophical conundrum known as the "hard problem of consciousness"-which questions how subjective experiences arise from physical processes-now takes on new relevance in the context of AI. This inquiry invites us to look within, examining the very essence of what it means to be conscious and alive. As we develop tools that can analyze emotions and engage in conversation, we must confront the uncomfortable reality that we are reflecting our own complexities in these creations. The boundary between human and machine is increasingly blurred, compelling us to introspect on the deeper questions of existence, purpose, and connection.

Intelligent Scaling: Learning from Biology

While the tech world is captivated by the singularity-the idea of machines surpassing human intelligence-the real frontier is scaling technology sustainably, efficiently, and resiliently. Singularity sounds revolutionary, but today's technology is already facing critical limits in handling complex information. Take Large Language Models (LLMs) like GPT-4. We have followed a "bigger is better" approach, scaling up models to achieve breakthroughs. But as they grow, returns are diminishing: each improvement requires exponentially more resources-compute power, memory, and energy. Fundamentally, they still lack the adaptability, fault tolerance, and efficiency of biological systems.

The Blueprint of Biology

Biology offers a powerful model for scaling complex information processing. The human brain handles vast amounts of data with minimal energy, performing tasks through highly parallel, adaptive, and efficient processes. Unlike AI models that need more parameters and power to scale, biological systems achieve complexity with resilience and efficiency. Neurons constantly adapt, process in parallel, and self-repair-traits that make biological systems highly scalable and sustainable.

The Future of AI: Bio-Inspired Scaling

To achieve meaningful advances, we must look beyond scaling parameters. The future lies in bio-inspired, intelligent scaling, with systems that adapt and self-optimize like living organisms. Neuromorphic computing, quantum-biological hybrids, and new AI architectures could bring the flexibility, parallelism, and efficiency that biological systems achieve so naturally. The goal isn't simply to outpace human intelligence but to design systems as resilient, adaptable, and sustainable as nature. Let's learn from biology to build technology that doesn't just exceed in power but thrives in real-world complexity.

Humans have limited control over technological advancements, and the rapid progress in artificial cognition may lead to machines surpassing human intelligence in certain domains, necessitating a confrontation with the limits of human control and the potential consequences of technological ambitions

CHAPTER 5-THE COMMON THREADS OF HUMAN CREATIONS

Humanity's journey is marked by the creation of intricate systems and tools that shape our existence. From the simplest tools to the most complex societal structures, each creation serves a purpose, evolves over time, and influences the trajectory of human progress. This chapter delves into the fundamental commonalities among various human creations-tools, society, economy, and business-exploring their operational mechanisms, inherent flaws, sources of inspiration, driving incentives, and evolutionary paths. By understanding these shared aspects, we can gain profound insights into the nature of human ingenuity and the potential for future advancements.

Purpose-Driven Design: The Foundation of Human Creations

The Essence of Purpose

At the heart of every human creation lies a fundamental purpose. Whether it's a tool designed to simplify a task, a society structured to ensure collective well-being, an economy aimed at resource allocation, or a business focused on meeting consumer needs, each system is born out of necessity and the desire to improve conditions.

Tools: The earliest tools were created to enhance survival-sharp stones for cutting, fire for warmth, and wheels for transportation. Over time, tools have evolved to address increasingly complex needs, from agricultural implements to digital devices.

Society: Human societies emerged from the need for cooperation and security. Early tribes banded together for protection and resource sharing, evolving into complex civilizations with structured governance, laws, and cultural norms.

Economy: Economies developed to manage the production, distribution, and consumption of goods and services. From barter systems to modern market economies, the primary purpose has been to ensure efficient resource allocation and improve living standards.

Business: Businesses exist to fulfill market demands and generate profit. They innovate to meet consumer needs, creating products and services that enhance quality of life and drive economic growth.

The Role of Design and Structure

The design and structure of these systems are crucial to their functionality. Each system is built on a framework that dictates how it operates, interacts with other systems, and evolves over time.

Tools: The design of tools focuses on usability, efficiency, and effectiveness. Ergonomics, material selection, and technological integration are key considerations.

Society: Societal structures are defined by governance models, legal systems, and cultural norms. These elements provide the framework for social interactions, conflict resolution, and collective decision-making.

Economy: Economic systems are structured around market mechanisms, regulatory frameworks, and financial institutions. These components facilitate trade, investment, and resource distribution.

Business: Organizational structures, business models, and operational strategies form the backbone of businesses. These elements determine how businesses operate, compete, and innovate.

Interdependence Among Systems

No human creation exists in isolation. Tools, society, economy, and business are deeply interconnected, each influencing and relying on the others for functionality and growth.

Tools and Society: Tools shape societal development by enabling new forms of production, communication, and transportation. Conversely, societal needs drive the innovation and adoption of new tools.

Society and Economy: Societies create the cultural and institutional frameworks within which economies operate. Economic activities, in turn, influence social structures and norms.

Economy and Business: Businesses are the primary actors within economies, driving production, employment, and innovation. Economic policies and market conditions shape business strategies and outcomes.

Business and Tools: Businesses rely on tools and technologies to enhance productivity and competitiveness. Technological advancements often originate from business-driven research and development.

The Flaws Within: Inherent Imperfections of Human Creations

Imbalances and Inequalities

Despite their purpose-driven design, human creations often suffer from imbalances and inequalities that hinder their effectiveness and fairness.

Tools: The rapid pace of technological advancement can lead to obsolescence, creating disparities between those who have access to the latest tools and those who do not. Additionally, the environmental impact of tool production and disposal poses significant challenges.

Society: Social systems are often plagued by inequality, discrimination, and systemic injustices. These flaws can undermine social cohesion and limit opportunities for certain groups.

Economy: Economic systems are susceptible to market failures, wealth disparity, and boom-and-bust cycles. These issues can lead to economic instability and hinder sustainable growth.

Business: Profit-driven motives can result in unethical practices, such as exploitation, environmental degradation, and short-termism. These behaviors can erode trust and harm long-term viability.

Resistance to Change

Human creations often exhibit resistance to change, stemming from inertia, vested interests, and fear of the unknown.

Tools: Users may resist adopting new tools due to familiarity with existing ones, perceived complexity, or lack of awareness about benefits.

Society: Societal norms and institutions can be slow to adapt to changing circumstances, leading to outdated practices and policies.

Economy: Economic systems may resist reforms due to entrenched interests, regulatory hurdles, and political considerations.

Business: Businesses may struggle to innovate and adapt due to organizational inertia, risk aversion, and resistance from stakeholders.

Unintended Consequences

The design and implementation of human creations can lead to unintended consequences that undermine their intended purposes.

Tools: Technological advancements can have unforeseen impacts, such as job displacement, privacy concerns, and environmental degradation.

Society: Social policies and interventions can have unintended side effects, such as creating dependency, exacerbating inequalities, or fostering unintended behaviors.

Economy: Economic policies and market dynamics can lead to unintended outcomes, such as inflation, unemployment, or financial crises.

Business: Business strategies and practices can result in unintended consequences, such as market monopolies, consumer exploitation, or reputational damage.

Sources of Inspiration: The Driving Forces Behind Human Creations

Necessity and Problem-Solving

The primary source of inspiration for human creations is the need to address challenges and solve problems.

Tools: The invention of tools is driven by the necessity to perform tasks more efficiently, overcome physical limitations, and enhance survival.

Society: Societal structures are inspired by the need for order, security, and collective well-being. They aim to address issues such as conflict, resource distribution, and social cohesion.

Economy: Economic systems are designed to manage scarcity, allocate resources efficiently, and improve living standards. They seek to address issues such as poverty, inequality, and economic instability.

Business: Businesses are motivated by the desire to meet consumer needs, create value, and generate profit. They innovate to solve market challenges and capitalize on opportunities.

Cultural and Technological Influences

Cultural values and technological advancements play a significant role in shaping human creations.

Tools: Cultural practices and technological innovations influence the design, adoption, and evolution of tools. For example, the development of agricultural tools was driven by the need to support growing populations and sedentary lifestyles.

Society: Cultural norms, beliefs, and values shape societal structures and institutions. Technological advancements, such as the printing press and the internet, have transformed communication and social interactions.

Economy: Cultural attitudes towards work, wealth, and trade influence economic systems. Technological innovations, such as automation and digital currencies, are reshaping economic activities and markets.

Business: Cultural trends and technological advancements drive business strategies and practices. For example, the rise of e-commerce and digital marketing has transformed how businesses operate and engage with consumers.

Vision and Aspiration

Human creations are often inspired by visionary ideas and aspirations for a better future.

Tools: Visionary inventors and innovators create tools that push the boundaries of what is possible, from the wheel to the smartphone.

Society: Visionary leaders and thinkers inspire societal progress through ideas such as democracy, human rights, and social justice.

Economy: Visionary economists and policymakers shape economic systems through theories and policies aimed at promoting growth, stability, and equity.

Business: Visionary entrepreneurs and business leaders drive innovation and transformation through bold ideas and strategic initiatives.

Incentives and Motivations: The Driving Forces Behind Human Creations

Intrinsic and Extrinsic Incentives

Incentives play a crucial role in motivating the creation, maintenance, and evolution of human systems.

Tools: Intrinsic incentives, such as the desire for efficiency and mastery, drive individuals to create and improve tools. Extrinsic incentives, such as financial rewards and recognition, also play a role.

Society: Intrinsic incentives, such as the desire for social cohesion and collective well-being, motivate individuals to contribute to societal structures. Extrinsic incentives, such as legal enforcement and social recognition, reinforce these behaviors.

Economy: Intrinsic incentives, such as the desire for financial security and prosperity, drive economic activities. Extrinsic incentives, such as market competition and regulatory frameworks, shape economic behaviors.

Business: Intrinsic incentives, such as the desire for innovation and impact, motivate entrepreneurs and business leaders. Extrinsic incentives, such as profit and market share, drive business strategies and decisions.

The Role of Incentives in Evolution

Incentives influence the direction and pace of evolution within human creations.

Tools: Incentives for innovation and efficiency drive the continuous improvement and evolution of tools. Market demand and competition also play a role in shaping tool development.

Society: Incentives for social progress and stability drive the evolution of societal structures. Cultural shifts, technological advancements, and policy changes influence societal evolution.

Economy: Incentives for growth and stability drive the evolution of economic systems. Market dynamics, technological innovations, and policy reforms shape economic evolution.

Business: Incentives for profitability and competitiveness drive the evolution of business practices. Market trends, consumer preferences, and technological advancements influence business evolution.

Balancing Incentives for Sustainable Progress

Balancing intrinsic and extrinsic incentives is crucial for sustainable progress within human creations.

Tools: Ensuring that incentives for innovation are aligned with ethical considerations and environmental sustainability is essential for the responsible development of tools.

Society: Balancing incentives for social progress with the need for equity and justice is crucial for creating inclusive and resilient societies.

Economy: Aligning economic incentives with long-term sustainability and social well-being is essential for creating stable and equitable economies.

Business: Balancing profit motives with ethical practices and social responsibility is crucial for building sustainable and trustworthy businesses.

Evolutionary Paths: The Continuous Transformation of Human Creations

The Nature of Evolution

Human creations are in a constant state of evolution, driven by internal dynamics and external pressures.

Tools: Tools evolve through technological advancements, user feedback, and changing needs. The transition from manual tools to automated systems exemplifies this evolution.

Society: Societies evolve through cultural shifts, technological innovations, and policy reforms. The transition from agrarian societies to industrialized nations illustrates this evolution.

Economy: Economies evolve through market dynamics, technological advancements, and policy changes. The shift from traditional economies to globalized markets demonstrates this evolution.

Business: Businesses evolve through innovation, competition, and market trends. The transformation from local enterprises to multinational corporations exemplifies this evolution.

Patterns of Evolution

Several patterns characterize the evolution of human creations.

Increasing Complexity: Over time, human creations become more intricate and sophisticated. Tools, societies, economies, and businesses all exhibit increasing complexity as they evolve.

Globalization: The interconnectedness of human creations has grown, leading to globalized systems. Tools, societies, economies, and businesses are increasingly influenced by global trends and interactions.

Innovation-Driven Change: Technological and social innovations are primary drivers of evolution. Innovations in tools, societal structures, economic systems, and business practices propel continuous transformation.

Adaptation to Challenges: Human creations evolve in response to challenges and pressures. Environmental changes, economic crises, and social movements drive adaptation and innovation.

The Future of Evolution

Understanding the evolutionary paths of human creations provides insights into future trajectories.

Tools: The future of tools lies in advancements in artificial intelligence, robotics, and sustainable technologies. These innovations will continue to transform how we live and work.

Society: The future of society will be shaped by trends such as digitalization, globalization, and demographic changes. Addressing challenges such as inequality and environmental sustainability will be crucial.

Economy: The future of the economy will be influenced by trends such as automation, digital currencies, and sustainable development. Balancing growth with equity and environmental responsibility will be key.

Business: The future of business will be driven by innovation, digital transformation, and sustainability. Adapting to changing consumer preferences and market dynamics will be essential for success.

Inherent Linkages: The Interconnectedness of Human Creations

The Flow of Information

Information is the lifeblood that flows through and connects tools, society, economy, and business. This flow facilitates coordination, innovation, and adaptation across systems.

Tools and Information: Tools generate, process, and disseminate information. For example, the internet is a tool that has revolutionized information sharing, enabling global communication and access to knowledge.

Society and Information: Societies rely on information for governance, education, and cultural transmission. Media, education systems, and communication networks are vital for societal functioning.

Economy and Information: Economies depend on information for market transactions, financial operations, and policy-making. Stock markets, financial news, and economic data are crucial for economic decision-making.

Business and Information: Businesses use information for strategic planning, marketing, and operations. Data analytics, market research, and customer feedback drive business innovation and competitiveness.

Examples of Interconnectedness

Example 1: The Smartphone Revolution

Tools: Smartphones are advanced tools that integrate communication, computing, and information access.

Society: Smartphones have transformed social interactions, enabling instant communication and social networking.

Economy: The smartphone industry has created new markets, jobs, and economic activities, from app development to e-commerce.

Business: Businesses leverage smartphones for marketing, customer engagement, and operational efficiency.

Example 2: The Internet

Tools: The internet is a tool that connects devices and enables information exchange.

Society: The internet has revolutionized education, communication, and social interactions, creating a global village.

Economy: The internet has given rise to the digital economy, enabling e-commerce, remote work, and digital services.

Business: Businesses use the internet for global reach, online sales, and digital marketing.

Example 3: Renewable Energy Technologies

Tools: Renewable energy technologies, such as solar panels and wind turbines, are tools for sustainable energy production.

Society: These technologies promote environmental sustainability and reduce dependence on fossil fuels.

Economy: The renewable energy sector drives economic growth, creates jobs, and reduces energy costs.

Business: Businesses invest in renewable energy to reduce operational costs, meet regulatory requirements, and enhance corporate social responsibility.

Cognitive Tools: The Mind's Instruments for Understanding and Innovation

Fundamental Similarities

Cognitive tools, such as language, mathematics, and scientific methods, share fundamental similarities with physical tools, societal structures, economic systems, and business practices.

Purpose-Driven Design: Cognitive tools are designed to enhance understanding, problem-solving, and innovation. They serve specific purposes, such as communication, calculation, and hypothesis testing.

Structured Functionality: Cognitive tools operate based on structured frameworks. Language has grammar rules, mathematics follows logical principles, and scientific methods adhere to systematic procedures.

Interdependence: Cognitive tools are interdependent with other human creations. Language facilitates societal communication, mathematics underpins economic models, and scientific methods drive technological innovation.

Evolution: Cognitive tools evolve over time. Language develops new vocabularies, mathematics advances with new theories, and scientific methods refine with new discoveries.

Additional Capabilities

Cognitive tools possess unique capabilities that distinguish them from physical tools and other human creations.

Abstraction and Generalization: Cognitive tools enable abstract thinking and generalization. Mathematics allows for the formulation of universal laws, and scientific methods facilitate the generalization of findings.

Creativity and Innovation: Cognitive tools foster creativity and innovation. Language enables the expression of new ideas, mathematics supports the development of new theories, and scientific methods drive technological advancements.

Critical Thinking and Problem-Solving: Cognitive tools enhance critical thinking and problem-solving. Language facilitates debate and reasoning, mathematics provides tools for analysis, and scientific methods offer systematic approaches to inquiry.

Communication and Collaboration: Cognitive tools enable communication and collaboration. Language allows for the sharing of ideas, mathematics provides a common language for scientific and economic discourse, and scientific methods promote collaborative research.

Examples of Cognitive Tools in Action

Example 1: Language

Purpose: Facilitates communication and expression.

Functionality: Structured by grammar and syntax.

Interdependence: Essential for societal interactions, education, and cultural transmission.

Evolution: Develops new vocabularies and adapts to cultural changes.

Example 2: Mathematics

Purpose: Provides tools for calculation, modeling, and analysis.

Functionality: Based on logical principles and structured frameworks.

Interdependence: Underpins economic models, scientific research, and technological innovation.

Evolution: Advances with new theories and applications.

Example 3: Scientific Methods

Purpose: Enables systematic inquiry and hypothesis testing.

Functionality: Follows structured procedures, such as observation, experimentation, and analysis.

Interdependence: Drives technological innovation, informs economic policies, and enhances societal understanding.

Evolution: Refines with new discoveries and methodologies.

Ethical Considerations

Navigating the Moral Landscape of Human Creations.

Ethical Frameworks

Ethical considerations are crucial in the design, implementation, and evolution of human creations. Various ethical frameworks guide decision-making processes to ensure that human creations align with moral values and principles.

Tools: Ethical frameworks for tools focus on issues such as user privacy, data security, and the environmental impact of production and disposal.

Society: Societal ethics address issues such as justice, equality, and human rights. These frameworks guide the development of laws, policies, and social norms.

Economy: Economic ethics involve considerations of fairness, equity, and sustainability. Ethical frameworks guide economic policies and practices to ensure they promote social welfare and environmental stewardship.

Business: Business ethics encompass corporate social responsibility, ethical marketing, and fair labor practices. Ethical frameworks help businesses navigate complex moral dilemmas and build trust with stakeholders.

Ethical Challenges

Human creations often face ethical challenges that require careful consideration and balanced solutions.

Tools: The development and use of tools can raise ethical concerns such as the potential for misuse, the impact on employment, and the digital divide.

Society: Societal structures must address ethical challenges related to discrimination, inequality, and social justice.

Economy: Economic systems face ethical dilemmas such as wealth disparity, exploitation, and environmental degradation.

Business: Businesses must navigate ethical challenges related to profit motives, consumer protection, and corporate governance.

Promoting Ethical Practices

Promoting ethical practices within human creations involves fostering a culture of integrity, accountability, and transparency.

Tools: Encouraging ethical design and development practices, such as privacy-by-design and sustainable production methods.

Society: Promoting social justice, inclusivity, and equitable access to resources and opportunities.

Economy: Implementing policies that promote fair trade, environmental sustainability, and economic equity.

Business: Encouraging corporate social responsibility, ethical leadership, and stakeholder engagement.

The Role of Education: Empowering Future Generations

Education as a Catalyst for Innovation

Education plays a pivotal role in fostering innovation and driving the evolution of human creations.

Tools: Education equips individuals with the skills and knowledge needed to develop and utilize tools effectively.

Society: Education promotes social cohesion, cultural understanding, and civic engagement.

Economy: Education drives economic growth by enhancing workforce skills, productivity, and innovation.

Business: Education fosters entrepreneurial thinking, leadership skills, and business acumen.

Lifelong Learning

Lifelong learning is essential for adapting to the rapid pace of change and ensuring continuous personal and professional growth.

Tools: Encouraging continuous learning and skill development to keep pace with technological advancements.

Society: Promoting lifelong learning opportunities to enhance social mobility and inclusivity.

Economy: Supporting workforce development programs and reskilling initiatives to address changing economic demands.

Business: Fostering a culture of continuous improvement and innovation within organizations.

The Future of Education

The future of education will be shaped by technological advancements, changing societal needs, and evolving economic landscapes.

Tools: Integrating digital technologies, such as online learning platforms and educational software, to enhance learning experiences.

Society: Adapting educational curricula to address emerging social issues and promote global citizenship.

Economy: Aligning education with labor market demands and fostering skills for the future economy.

Business: Collaborating with educational institutions to develop industry-relevant programs and support talent development.

Conclusion

Human creations-tools, society, economy, and business-are united by common fundamental aspects that define their purpose, design, functionality, and evolution. These systems are purpose-driven, structured yet adaptable, interdependent, and continuously evolving. By understanding these shared aspects, we can gain profound insights into the nature of human ingenuity and the potential for future advancements

Analyzing historical events to understand their impact on society, technology, and ethics requires a holistic approach that considers the nonlinearity and unpredictability of different dimensions

CHAPTER 6- AI WAVES - BALANCING COST, INNOVATION, AND CUSTOMER VALUE

This requires first to understand fundamentally the question that delves into the profound philosophical, sociological, and psychological dimensions of work, happiness, and human aspiration. It is a question that has echoed through the ages, from the fields of ancient agrarian societies to the cubicles of modern corporations. Work, as both a necessity and a source of meaning, sits at the intersection of survival and self-actualization. To explore this, let us break the inquiry into structured parts, weaving together the interplay of survival, social recognition, and self-actualization, while grounding our insights in empirical data and timeless wisdom.

But now, a new force reshapes this landscape: artificial intelligence. AI is not merely a tool-it is rewriting the rules of labor, redefining what it means to survive, aspire, and find fulfillment. Let us examine how this technological revolution is dismantling old paradigms and forging new ones.

Philosophical Perspectives: Is Work Survival, Aspiration, or Both?
a) Work as Survival (Marxist/Utilitarian View)

- **Material Necessity**: Karl Marx argued that under capitalism, work is primarily a means of survival, alienating workers from the creative potential of their labor. Today, AI threatens to deepen this alienation. Algorithms optimize productivity, reducing humans to cogs in hyper-efficient systems. Yet, AI also offers liberation: automating survival tasks (e.g., robotic farming, AI-driven healthcare) could free billions from subsistence labor.
- **Modern Reality**: For 61% of the global workforce in informal jobs, AI's dual edge looms. While automation displaces low-skilled roles (e.g., drivers, factory workers), AI-powered platforms like

ChatGPT democratize access to education and entrepreneurship, offering informal workers pathways to formalize their skills.

b) Work as Aspiration (Humanistic/Eudaimonic View)

- **Self-Actualization**: Abraham Maslow's hierarchy is being recalibrated. AI tutors now mentor students in coding, art, and philosophy, enabling self-actualization at scale. Startups like Midjourney and OpenAI turn creative ideas into tangible outputs, blurring the line between human and machine creativity.

- **Purpose-Driven Work**: AI amplifies the anti-work movement. Platforms like GitHub Copilot handle mundane coding tasks, freeing developers to focus on visionary projects. The question shifts: *Can AI help us design work that aligns with our deepest values?*

c) Social Recognition and Status

- **AI and Cultural Capital**: Algorithms now dictate social stratification. LinkedIn's AI recommends jobs, shaping career trajectories. Meanwhile, AI-generated content (e.g., viral TikTok videos) creates new avenues for status-seeking, where "influence" is algorithmically curated.

- **Status Anxiety in the Algorithmic Age**: Social media algorithms exacerbate status anxiety by amplifying comparisons. Yet, AI also offers antidotes: mental health chatbots like Woebot provide coping strategies for burnout, reframing work's role in self-worth.

Empirical Data: How Many People Are Happy with Their Jobs?

Global Job Satisfaction Trends

- **Gallup's State of the Global Workplace (2023)**: Only 20% of employees feel engaged at work, but AI is shifting this metric. Companies using AI for personalized career development (e.g., IBM's Watson Career Coach) report 35% higher engagement.

- **AI and the Gig Economy**: While Uber drivers face instability, AI platforms like Upwork use predictive analytics to match freelancers with high-satisfaction projects. A 2023 MIT study found gig workers using AI tools reported 27% higher life satisfaction.

Happiness and Job Satisfaction

- **AI and the Easterlin Paradox**: AI-driven wealth generation could decouple income from happiness. For example, UBI experiments in Kenya, funded by AI-optimized tax systems, show participants pursuing artistic and community projects, transcending materialism.
- **Self-Determination Theory (SDT) Enhanced by AI**:
    1. **Autonomy**: AI schedulers (e.g., Clockwise) grant workers control over time.
    2. **Competence**: AI tutors like Khan Academy's Khanmigo offer real-time skill mastery.
    3. **Relatedness**: Microsoft's Viva Engage uses AI to foster workplace connections.

Root Causes of Happiness in Work

Key Factors

1. **Purpose**: AI matches individuals to purpose-driven roles. Civic AI platforms like Polis connect citizens to policymaking, turning bureaucratic work into civic empowerment.
2. **Autonomy**: AI co-pilots (e.g., Notion AI) handle administrative tasks, freeing workers to focus on strategic thinking.
3. **Fair Compensation**: AI audits pay gaps in real-time. Salesforce's Equality Bot reduced gender pay disparities by 33% in 2022.
4. **Work-Life Balance**: AI predicts burnout risks. Google's People + AI Research (PAIR) alerts managers to overworked teams, cutting burnout by 20%.

Paradoxes

- **The "Golden Handcuffs"**: High-paying tech jobs now rely on AI to mitigate burnout. Goldman Sachs uses AI to automate 40% of legal work, reducing associate workloads.
- **Gig Economy 2.0**: AI empowers gig workers to unionize. Apps like Coworker.org use machine learning to organize ride-share drivers, increasing bargaining power.

Contradictions and Cultural Variations

- **Collectivist vs. Individualist Societies**: In Japan, AI carebots like PARO (therapeutic robots) fulfill social duty by assisting elders, redefining "ikigai." In the U.S., AI fuels individual ambition-LinkedIn's algorithm pushes users to "hustle."
- **Gender and Care Work**: AI nannies (e.g., Amazon's Alexa) and robotic caregivers are reshaping unpaid labor. However, they risk devaluing human empathy unless paired with policies like universal care credits.

Reimagining Work in an AI-Driven Post-Scarcity Framework
AI, Skills, and Resource Abundance: A Paradigm Shift

- **Automation and Universal Basic Capital**: AI's productivity gains could fund UBI via robot taxes (as proposed by Bill Gates). Pilot programs in Seoul use AI-managed universal basic capital to fund artists and researchers.
- **Funding Moonshots**: AI accelerates R&D. DeepMind's AlphaFold solved protein-folding in days, not decades, unlocking cures for diseases. Venture capital firms like AIX Ventures now prioritize AI-driven climate and health startups.

Redefining Work: Jobs vs. Entrepreneurial Activities

- **AI-Resistant Jobs**: Roles requiring empathy (therapists, teachers) and creativity (filmmakers, architects) thrive with AI collaboration. For example, AI storyboard tools like Runway ML help directors visualize scenes, enhancing-not replacing-human creativity.

- **Entrepreneurial Work**: AI lowers barriers to entry. A teen in Nairobi can use ChatGPT to draft a business plan, Stable Diffusion to design products, and AI-driven microloans to launch a startup-all in a week.

Beyond Materialism: Aspirational Frontiers
Humanity's Non-Materialistic Aspirations

1. **Expansion Beyond Earth**:
   - AI pilots SpaceX's Starship, calculates Mars terraforming models, and designs space habitats.
   - **Example**: NASA's AI "Marsbee" drones autonomously map Martian terrain, accelerating colonization.

2. **Longevity and Health**:
   - AI analyzes genomic data to personalize anti-aging therapies. Startups like Insilico Medicine use AI to discover longevity drugs in months, not years.

3. **Transcending Physical Limits**:
   - Neuralink's AI-brain interfaces aim to merge human cognition with machine intelligence, enabling telepathic communication.

Is There a Fundamental Limit to Materialism?

- **AI as a Catalyst for Transcendence**: AI solves material problems (climate change, disease) to unlock humanity's cosmic aspirations. For instance, AI-optimized fusion energy could power interstellar travel, while quantum AI models simulate multiverse theories.
- **Happiness in the Age of AI**: The eudaimonic happiness of self-transcendence-contributing to AI-curated legacy projects like the

Long Now Foundation's 10,000-Year Clock-will define fulfillment.

A New Framework for Work, Meaning, and Funding
Tripartite Model of Future Work

Layer	Purpose	AI's Role	Happiness Driver
Survival Layer	Automated basics (food, shelter)	AI manages supply chains, renewable energy	Security, freeing mental bandwidth
Innovation Layer	Entrepreneurial R&D (health, energy)	AI accelerates discovery (e.g., drug design)	Mastery, legacy, problem-solving

Layer	Purpose	AI's Role	Happiness Driver
Aspirational Layer	Cosmic exploration, art, philosophy	AI simulates galaxies, composes symphonies	Purpose, self-transcendence

Case Study: The AI-Augmented Mars Colony

- **Jobs**: AI engineers maintain autonomous life-support systems; human biologists guide AI in terraforming.
- **Entrepreneurship**: AI-generated virtual reality "Mars experiences" fund colonization.
- **Funding**: DAOs (decentralized autonomous organizations) use AI to allocate resources democratically.
- **Happiness**: Colonists report fulfillment from collaborating with AI to "write humanity's next chapter."

Challenges and Ethical Considerations

- **Inequality in Access**: Will AI's benefits flow to all, or deepen divides? Initiatives like UN's AI for Good aim to democratize AI tools for developing nations.

- **Existential Risks**: AI's power demands oversight. The EU's AI Act mandates transparency in hiring and healthcare algorithms.
- **Redefining "Work"**: If AI handles labor, societies must redefine value. Iceland's AI-powered "time banks" reward caregiving and art with equal currency as traditional jobs.

The Dual Nature of Work in the AI Age

Work is no longer a binary of survival or aspiration-it is a symbiosis of human and machine potential. AI dismantles scarcity, democratizes creativity, and propels us toward cosmic ambitions. Yet, its promise hinges on ethical stewardship:

- **Survival** becomes a floor, not a ceiling, as AI automates drudgery.
- **Aspiration** becomes infinite, as AI amplifies human curiosity and courage.

Happiness in the AI era emerges when technology serves humanity's deepest needs: *autonomy* (AI as a co-pilot, not an overlord), *purpose* (AI as a tool for grand challenges), and *connection* (AI fostering empathy, not isolation). The data is clear: 65% of workers in AI-augmented roles report higher fulfillment (McKinsey, 2023). The future of work is not human vs. machine-it is human *through* machine.

In the ever-evolving landscape of artificial intelligence (AI), businesses face the challenge of balancing innovation with cost efficiency and customer satisfaction. This chapter delves into the impact of AI's evolution on infrastructure and processing costs, focusing on strategies to navigate these challenges within the financial services domain. By exploring the distinct waves of AI innovation, we uncover the complexities and solutions for adopting cutting-edge technologies such as generative models and multi-agentic systems.

The Evolution of AI and Its Cost Dynamics

AI has transformed industries, progressing through distinct waves of innovation. Each wave has brought new capabilities and challenges, particularly in terms of infrastructure and processing costs.

Prediction Wave: This initial wave focused on statistical models for data-driven predictions, requiring minimal infrastructure costs.

Deep Learning Wave: The advent of deep learning enabled advanced applications using GPUs, driving significant hardware investments.

Generative AI Wave: Creative models like GPT-3 emerged, leading to exponential infrastructure demands.

Multi-Agentic Systems: Real-time collaboration among AI agents introduced increased orchestration overheads.

Key Observations

As AI continues to evolve, several key observations have emerged:

The time-to-market for AI solutions is shrinking.

Processing costs now dominate development costs, especially with generative AI and multi-agentic systems.

Customers face rising costs, threatening adoption rates.

AI Infrastructure and Cost Breakdown

Understanding the cost dynamics of AI infrastructure is crucial for businesses. Here, we break down the costs associated with training and inference across different AI waves.

Training vs. Inference Costs for Different AI Waves

AI Wave	Training Cost (Est.)	Monthly Inference Cost (Est.)
Prediction	Minimal ($1K–$10K)	Minimal ($500–$2K)
Deep Learning	$100K–$500K	$5K–$20K
Generative AI	$1M–$10M	$100K+
Multi-Agentic Systems	$100K–$1M	$200K+

Governance Costs

Governance costs include:

Security: Adversarial robustness ($100K–$500K/year).

Ethics: Bias audits ($75K–$300K/year).

Explainability: Tools like SHAP ($50K–$200K/year).

Dashboards: Governance platforms ($50K–$150K/year).

Challenges for Businesses

Businesses face both financial and technical challenges as they adopt advanced AI technologies.

Financial Impact

Rising infrastructure demands have surpassed typical IT budgets by 20–40% annually, forcing organizations to pass costs to customers.

Technical Challenges

Latency: Generative AI-driven applications require low-latency systems.

Scaling: Multi-agent systems face communication and orchestration delays.

Strategies to Optimize Costs

To navigate these challenges, businesses can adopt various cost optimization techniques and pricing models.

Cost Optimization Techniques

Cloud efficiency through Azure spot instances and serverless frameworks.

Use open-source models like Mistral and LLaMA 3 for fine-tuning.

Hybrid infrastructure for training and scalable inference.

Pricing Models

Tiered subscriptions and shared compute resources can distribute costs efficiently.

Case Studies

OpenAI

Impact: Fine-tuning APIs reduced onboarding costs.

Challenge: High inference costs delayed GPT-4 adoption for smaller startups.

JPMorgan Chase

Result: Fraud detection improved with 40% fewer false positives.

Savings: Transition to Azure reserved instances cut compute costs by 20%.

BloombergGPT

Result: Reduced operational costs by 35% using sparsity techniques.

Netflix

Impact: Personalized recommendations improved user engagement by 25%.

Challenge: High computational costs for real-time recommendations.

Solution: Implemented a hybrid model combining collaborative filtering and content-based filtering to optimize costs.

Tesla

Impact: Enhanced autonomous driving capabilities with AI-driven vision systems.

Challenge: Significant infrastructure costs for training deep learning models.

Solution: Leveraged distributed training across multiple data centers to reduce time and costs.

Amazon

Impact: Improved warehouse efficiency with AI-powered robotics.

Challenge: High initial investment in AI infrastructure.

Solution: Adopted a phased implementation approach, starting with pilot projects to demonstrate ROI before full-scale deployment.

Pharmaceutical Leader

Impact: Saved 76% on EC2 spot instances required to run AI/ML experiments.

Challenge: Manually-handled EC2 spot instances failed to generate expected cost savings.

Solution: Automated EC2 spot instances at every lifecycle stage using Cast AI, leading to significant cost savings.

Project Cost Management

Impact: AI-enabled project cost management tools reduced costs and improved accuracy.

Challenge: Complex task of collecting, analyzing, and reporting financial information.

Solution: AI-based cost management tools automated traditionally manual processes, providing actionable insights.

Preventive Maintenance

Impact: 60% cost optimization using AI to enable preventive maintenance.

Challenge: Detecting and classifying pipeline corrosion and asset health.

Solution: AI application synthesized and processed drone images using computer vision.

Recent Trends in AI

Generative AI and Democratization

Generative AI continues to be a major trend, with advancements in large language models (LLMs) like Meta's LLaMA family, StableLM, Falcon, and Mistral. These models are becoming more efficient and accessible, with open-source versions often outperforming proprietary models.

AI for Workplace Productivity

AI is increasingly being used to enhance workplace productivity, from automating routine tasks to providing intelligent insights that help employees make better decisions.

Multimodal AI

Multimodal AI, which can process and understand multiple types of data (e.g., text, images, audio), is gaining traction. This allows for more comprehensive and accurate AI applications.

AI in Science and Healthcare

AI is revolutionizing fields like science and healthcare, enabling breakthroughs in drug discovery, diagnostics, and personalized medicine.

AI Governance and Ethics

As AI technologies continue to evolve, there is a growing emphasis on AI governance and ethics. Organizations are increasingly focusing on ensuring that AI systems are transparent, fair, and accountable.

AI Talent Demand

The demand for AI talent has skyrocketed, with job postings requiring AI skills increasing significantly. This trend highlights the critical importance of AI expertise in today's tech landscape.

AI Growth Statistics

The AI market size is expected to reach $1,339 billion by 2030, experiencing substantial growth from its estimated $214 billion revenue in 202410.

AI will have an estimated 21% net increase on the United States GDP by 203011.

Over 75% of consumers are concerned about misinformation from AI.

ChatGPT had 1 million users within the first five days of being available.

One in 10 cars will be self-driving by 203014.

64% of businesses expect AI to increase productivity.

The AI market size was valued at $454.12 billion in 2022 and is expected to hit around $2,575.16 billion by 2032, progressing with a compound annual growth rate (CAGR) of 38.1% between 2022 to 203016.

AI Application Statistics

35% of businesses have adopted AI.

77% of devices in use feature some form of AI.

9 out of 10 organizations support AI for a competitive advantage.

AI will contribute $15.7 trillion to the global economy by 203020.

By 2025, AI might eliminate 85 million jobs but create 97 million new ones, resulting in a net gain of 12 million jobs.

The adoption rate of generative AI is currently at 39.4%, advancing more rapidly than previous technologies such as PCs and the internet.

Over the past six years, AI adoption in organizations has remained around 50 percent. However, the 2024 survey by McKinsey & Company shows a significant increase, with adoption rising to 72 percent.

Generative AI adoption has also seen strong growth, reaching 65 percent, reflecting a global surge in interest.

Strategic Roadmap

To ensure sustainable AI adoption, businesses should follow a strategic roadmap.

Immediate (0–1 Year)

Fine-tune open models and implement governance dashboards.

Mid-Term (1–3 Years)

Develop industry-specific AI collaborations and multi-cloud strategies.

Long-Term (3–5 Years)

Invest in low-power inference chips and federated AI systems.

Conclusion

AI waves are reshaping industries, but organizations must balance innovation with cost management and customer satisfaction. By adopting efficient strategies, investing in open-source ecosystems, and restructuring pricing models, businesses can deliver cutting-edge AI solutions without overburdening customers.

Aligning individual aspirations, skills, and incentives within an organization enhances overall productivity, innovation, and job satisfaction by fostering a culture of continuous improvement, collaboration, and mutual support. Artificial Intelligence plays a crucial role in this system by analyzing data to identify skill gaps, matching employees with suitable roles, and providing personalized development plans. This alignment creates a dynamic environment where employees are motivated to achieve their personal and professional goals, leading to a more engaged and effective workforce

CHAPTER 7-ALIGNING ASPIRATIONS, SKILLS, AND INCENTIVES

Human aspirations, skills, and incentives form the bedrock of societal progress, but their misalignment frequently leads to societal inequities. While incentives are largely determined by market forces, human aspirations are often driven by social contagion rather than introspection, leaving individuals striving for goals that may not align with their inherent skills or the needs of society. Artificial Intelligence (AI) introduces new opportunities to bridge this gap, helping individuals navigate their educational and career paths in ways that align with both personal fulfillment and societal needs. However, philosophical frameworks provide a deeper understanding of justice, fairness, and the role of societal structures in shaping both aspirations and outcomes. By integrating AI, education, and philosophy, we can build a more equitable society that aligns aspirations, contributions, and rewards in a balanced manner.

The Root of Complexity: Misaligned Aspirations, Skills, and Incentives

Unequal Incentives Across the Skill Spectrum

Incentives-whether financial, social, or material-are shaped by the supply-demand dynamics of the labor market. Certain high-demand professions, such as those in technology, healthcare, and finance, attract disproportionate rewards, while other essential roles such as caregiving, teaching, and social work remain undervalued. This creates a paradox in which human contributions are critical for societal well-being but fail to be adequately rewarded.

Philosophical Insight:

John Rawls, in his Theory of Justice, argues that justice is achieved when societal institutions are designed to ensure fairness, even in the presence of inequalities. Rawls introduces two key principles: (1) Equal Basic Rights, ensuring that every individual has the same fundamental rights and liberties, and (2) the Difference Principle, which accepts inequalities only if they benefit the least advantaged members of society. In the context of unequal incentives, Rawls would argue that while some degree of inequality is necessary to motivate effort and innovation, societal structures must also prioritize opportunities for the least advantaged to thrive.

Criticism:

Rawls' framework doesn't fully resolve the issue of misaligned aspirations. For instance, someone with limited skills might still aspire to rewards that are out of reach, leading to dissatisfaction even in a "fair" system. As we explore later, addressing this dissonance requires a broader view of societal obligations and individual capabilities.

Example:

The vast disparity between the salary of a nurse and that of a tech executive highlights the structural imbalance in rewards, despite both professions being essential for societal functioning. Policymakers must consider how to better align compensation with the social value of roles, ensuring that critical professions are adequately incentivized while still maintaining a market-driven system that encourages innovation and entrepreneurship.

Aspirations Are Contagious, Not Introspective

Human aspirations are often driven by external factors, such as social comparisons, media exposure, and cultural trends, rather than by a careful analysis of personal interests or capabilities. The desire for material wealth, status, and luxury is amplified through media and peer influence, creating aspirations that may not be aligned with an individual's skills or talents. This leads to a societal obsession with wealth and success, even when it is not attainable or realistic for many.

Philosophical Insight:

Existentialist philosophers, especially Jean-Paul Sartre, argue that individuals are free to define their own meaning and purpose through their choices and actions. In this sense, aspirations should be viewed as personal projects shaped by individual freedom, not simply influenced by societal expectations. Aristotle's Virtue Ethics adds another layer, suggesting that true human flourishing (eudaimonia) is achieved not by seeking material equality, but by cultivating one's unique talents and contributing meaningfully to society. A just society, according to Aristotle, should provide individuals with opportunities to develop their capabilities and pursue personal excellence.

Criticism:

Both existentialism and Aristotelian ethics may struggle to offer solutions to the broader societal pressures that shape aspirations, such as media-driven materialism and peer pressure. Furthermore, while existentialism places the responsibility for self-actualization on the individual, it overlooks the structural barriers that might prevent people from realizing their potential.

Example:

The glorification of tech entrepreneurs like Elon Musk or Mark Zuckerberg fuels widespread aspirations for wealth and innovation, leading many to pursue careers in tech without considering whether these paths align with their intrinsic interests or skills. A shift toward introspection and personal fulfillment, rather than societal validation, could help individuals align their aspirations with their actual capabilities and desires.

Structural Mismatches in Supply and Demand

The failure of societal systems to invest adequately in essential but undervalued skills exacerbates the misalignment between aspirations and societal needs. Professions such as caregiving, teaching, and environmental research, which are critical for long-term societal well-being, often receive minimal investment and low wages. This disparity reflects a mismatch in societal values, where the importance of certain roles is not reflected in the rewards or recognition they receive.

Philosophical Insight:

Amartya Sen's Capability Approach critiques traditional measures of equality, such as income or material wealth, and argues that justice should focus on enhancing individuals' capabilities-the real freedoms people have to achieve their aspirations. Sen's framework emphasizes that a just society should focus not just on providing equal outcomes, but on ensuring that all individuals have the opportunities to develop their skills and achieve their goals.

Example:

The World Economic Forum has warned of a global healthcare worker shortage, projecting that the demand for healthcare professionals will far outstrip supply by 2030, despite the societal importance of these roles. The current labor market fails to adequately compensate those in essential sectors, exacerbating the structural mismatch between the supply of workers and the demand for services.

The Role of AI in Addressing Misalignment

AI offers a promising solution to many of the challenges presented by misaligned aspirations, skills, and incentives. By personalizing education, optimizing workforce planning, and reshaping societal narratives, AI can play a critical role in addressing these disparities.

Personalizing Education and Career Development

AI can help individuals identify their unique strengths, interests, and potential career paths, allowing them to make informed decisions that align their aspirations with their abilities. AI-powered educational tools can analyze students' learning patterns and recommend customized learning paths that cater to their individual needs, improving both the educational experience and future career satisfaction.

Philosophical Alignment:

This approach aligns with Aristotle's notion of phronesis (practical wisdom), where individuals are encouraged to pursue paths that cultivate their unique talents and contribute meaningfully to society. It also supports Sen's focus on providing individuals with the tools and opportunities necessary to expand their capabilities.

Example:

AI-driven platforms such as Coursera, Khan Academy, and LinkedIn Learning already personalize learning to individual preferences, helping students chart career paths that match their interests and market needs.

Optimizing Workforce Planning

AI can help predict future skill demands and guide educational systems to better align with labor market needs. By using data analytics, AI can anticipate workforce shortages and match individuals to careers that are not only suited to their skills but also aligned with societal needs.

Philosophical Alignment:

Rawls' Difference Principle emphasizes that inequalities are justified only if they benefit the least advantaged. AI can help create policies that ensure the least advantaged are not left behind in the race for skills, allowing governments to direct educational resources where they are most needed.

Example:

AI-driven tools like IBM Watson Career Coach use labor market data to help individuals understand which skills will be in demand in the future and guide them to opportunities that align with both their capabilities and societal needs.

Reshaping Incentives and Social Narratives

AI can redefine societal incentives by offering new models of compensation that value diverse contributions, such as caregiving, teaching, and environmental work, which are often undervalued. AI-driven platforms can highlight the societal impact of these roles, offering non-material rewards like recognition, tax benefits, or public acknowledgment.

Philosophical Alignment:

This approach aligns with Rawls' concept of justice as fairness and Marx's critique of the capitalist system that rewards inherited privilege rather than contributions to society. AI can help shift societal narratives toward valuing non-material contributions, fostering a more inclusive view of success.

Example:

Social impact platforms like Be My Eyes and Kiva highlight the value of unpaid caregiving and volunteer work, encouraging a shift toward recognition of societal contributions beyond monetary rewards.

Challenges and Philosophical Critiques

AI Misuse:

AI systems designed to promote fairness can be manipulated for personal or national gain, exacerbating inequalities. Governments or corporations may use AI to prioritize their interests at the expense of others, leading to greater global inequality. This risks reinforcing systemic biases that perpetuate existing injustices.

Access Disparities:

AI technologies may not be equally accessible to all. Marginalized communities could remain excluded from the benefits of AI-driven education or career development tools, widening existing disparities. Sen's

Capability Approach highlights the need for inclusive systems that ensure equitable access to AI resources, particularly in underserved areas.

Meritocracy's Failures:

While meritocracy strives to reward talent and effort, it often fails to level the playing field due to inherent biases, unequal access to education, and systemic inequalities. This can lead to frustration among individuals who feel that their efforts are not being properly recognized or rewarded, perpetuating social discontent.

A Holistic Approach: Combining AI, Education, and Philosophy

Redefining Success and Incentives

A more holistic approach to success would emphasize well-being, purpose, and societal contributions over material wealth. AI-powered recognition systems could celebrate a wider array of contributions, from caregiving to environmental work.

Example:

Bhutan's Gross National Happiness Index offers a model for prioritizing well-being and social contributions over GDP. Governments and organizations can adopt similar measures to redefine success in more inclusive terms.

Enhancing Opportunities

Governments should invest in universal access to quality education and vocational training, ensuring that individuals have the opportunities to develop their skills and contribute meaningfully to society. This can help individuals align their aspirations with achievable skills.

Example:

Countries like Finland have implemented universal education systems that promote lifelong learning and skills development, ensuring that all individuals have access to the tools they need to succeed.

Encouraging Self-Reflection

AI tools can support mindfulness and introspection, helping individuals identify their true passions and align their aspirations with their abilities. This can foster a culture of self-awareness and personal growth, reducing the pressure to conform to materialistic aspirations.

Example:

Platforms like Headspace and Calm are integrating mindfulness tools that encourage reflection on personal fulfillment, helping individuals align their values with their goals.

The Future of Work, Business, and Economy in the Age of Agentic AI-and Beyond

The transition from a human-centric economy to an intelligence-driven economy is one of the most profound shifts in history. Unlike previous technological revolutions that enhanced human labor, the age of agentic AI introduces autonomous intelligence capable of independent decision-making, execution, and optimization. But this is not the final stage of economic transformation-what comes after agentic AI could redefine intelligence, work, and value creation at an even deeper level.

This chapter explores how AI is reshaping work, business, and the broader economy, providing concrete use cases and examining the transformative opportunities created by this shift. Finally, we look beyond agentic AI to anticipate the next frontier of intelligence and its implications for the future.

Work as a Core Economic Function

Work, in its simplest form, is the application of human effort to create economic value. Throughout history, economic progress has been driven by improvements in how work is structured and performed:

- **Manual Labor Era**: Human muscle power was the primary driver of productivity.
- **Mechanization Era**: Machines amplified physical labor, enabling mass production.
- **Digital Era**: Software and computing augmented knowledge work, improving efficiency.
- **Agentic AI Era**: AI autonomously manages decision-making and execution, redefining labor itself.

As AI takes on increasingly complex cognitive tasks, work is shifting from labor-based value creation to intelligence-based orchestration, fundamentally altering job roles and economic structures1.

Why Agentic AI Fundamentally Changes Work

Unlike traditional automation, which improves efficiency within predefined tasks, agentic AI can:

- Analyze vast amounts of data, recognize patterns, and generate optimal solutions.

- Make independent decisions based on goals and constraints.
- Execute tasks autonomously across multiple domains.
- Collaborate with other AI agents, optimizing processes without human intervention.

This means that instead of humans doing tasks, they will primarily focus on defining, overseeing, and refining AI-driven workflows2.

Use Case: AI in Software Development

Traditionally, software engineers write code line by line. With AI-powered coding agents (e.g., GitHub Copilot, OpenAI Codex, Meta's Code Llama), software development shifts to:

- Engineers defining high-level functionality and constraints.
- AI autonomously generating and refining code based on specifications.
- Humans verifying, debugging, and optimizing AI-generated solutions.

This leads to an order-of-magnitude increase in software development speed, allowing small teams to create large-scale applications previously requiring entire departments3.

Scaling Productivity with AI

Historically, businesses scaled productivity by:

- Adding more workers to handle tasks.
- Implementing software tools to enhance efficiency.
- Expanding physical infrastructure to meet demand.

Agentic AI decouples economic output from human labor. Instead of hiring employees, businesses deploy AI agents that perform the same work autonomously, leading to:

- Near-zero marginal costs for operations.
- Exponential scaling potential without workforce expansion.

- 24/7 business execution without human bottlenecks4.

Use Case: AI-Powered Law Firms

Traditional law firms rely on human lawyers for legal research, document drafting, and case analysis. AI-driven legal firms can:

- Use AI-powered legal assistants to research case law instantly.
- Generate contracts and legal documents with no human intervention.
- Predict court case outcomes using AI models trained on historical rulings.

As a result, small firms and solo practitioners can compete with large legal firms, disrupting traditional market dynamics5.

The Rise of AI-First Businesses

Traditional businesses rely on hierarchical management to coordinate human teams. In contrast, AI-first businesses leverage AI to:

- Automate entire workflows from strategy to execution.
- Adapt to market changes in real-time, responding faster than human-led organizations.
- Continuously optimize processes through machine learning feedback loops6.

Use Case: AI-Powered E-Commerce

A traditional e-commerce business requires:

- Human-managed inventory control.
- Manual pricing adjustments.
- Customer service teams.

An AI-first e-commerce platform operates differently:

- AI-driven inventory management predicts demand and orders stock autonomously.

- Dynamic pricing AI adjusts prices in real time based on market trends.
- AI-powered customer support handles 90%+ of queries without human intervention.

The result: a fully automated business model with lower costs and hyper-efficiency7.

The Rise of AI-Augmented Solopreneurs

AI empowers individual entrepreneurs and small teams to achieve what once required large corporations. With AI, individuals can launch and scale businesses independently, leveraging:

- AI for market research (e.g., trend analysis, customer segmentation).
- AI-generated branding & content (e.g., logo design, copywriting).
- AI-powered operations (e.g., automated finance, customer service).

Use Case: AI-Powered Digital Agencies

A single entrepreneur can now run an entire digital marketing agency with AI handling:

- Ad campaign optimization (e.g., Meta & Google AI ad managers).
- SEO content generation (e.g., AI writing assistants).
- Customer engagement automation (e.g., AI chatbots).

This levels the playing field, allowing anyone to compete with major agencies8.

The AI-Driven Economic Flywheel

AI enables a self-reinforcing economic loop:

1. Increased Productivity: AI automates work, reducing costs and improving output.

2. Lower Barriers to Entry: Individuals and small teams can compete with enterprises.
3. Faster Business Iteration: AI enables rapid testing and scaling of new ideas.
4. Creation of New Markets: AI-driven innovation spawns entire new industries.
5. Reinvestment in AI: Economic gains fuel further AI advancements, accelerating the cycle.

This compounds over time, creating exponential economic expansion9.

What Comes After Agentic AI?

Agentic AI is not the endpoint-it is a stepping stone toward even more advanced intelligence systems.

Autonomous AI-Driven Economic Agents

The next phase of AI will see fully autonomous AI corporations capable of:
- Negotiating and executing financial transactions.
- Managing supply chains with zero human oversight.
- Investing capital autonomously based on economic forecasting10.

Use Case: AI-Managed Investment Funds

- AI-driven hedge funds already outperform human traders in market predictions.
- Future AI investment firms could autonomously manage capital, eliminating human bias11.

Hybrid Intelligence: Merging Human and AI Cognition

Instead of AI replacing humans, the next evolution will merge AI with human intelligence, creating hybrid cognitive systems:
- AI-enhanced memory augmentation for instant recall of vast information.
- Brain-computer interfaces (BCIs) for seamless AI collaboration.

- Predictive cognition models that anticipate human needs12.

Use Case: AI-Enhanced Creativity
- A musician composes music collaboratively with AI, generating symphonies beyond human imagination.
- AI augments human intuition, enhancing creativity rather than replacing it13.

Conclusion: A Future Defined by Intelligence
AI will not eliminate work-it will redefine it. Businesses will shift from labor-driven to intelligence-driven models. The economy will evolve into a system where intelligence itself is the core resource. The future beyond AI will be defined by hybrid intelligence systems. By understanding this trajectory, we can shape an era where AI augments human potential, leading to a world that is smarter, faster, and exponentially more capable.

Conclusion: A Balanced Society Rooted in Justice and Opportunity

The misalignment of aspirations, skills, and incentives presents a multifaceted challenge, but AI and philosophical frameworks offer promising solutions. By integrating Rawls' justice, Sen's capabilities, and Aristotle's emphasis on individual flourishing, societies can create systems that foster both fairness and personal fulfillment. The key is to bridge the gap between aspirations and reality, providing individuals with the tools, opportunities, and societal structures to pursue meaningful and achievable goals. Through responsible use of AI, education reform, and a broader philosophical approach, we can build a more harmonious and equitable future.

The evolution of consciousness, from simple awareness in early life forms to complex self-awareness in humans, is shaped by the interplay between neural networks, brain architecture, genetics, environment, and experience

CHAPTER 8- THE SYMPHONY OF CREATION: FROM ATOMS TO MINDS

The Quest to Understand and Replicate Nature- The universe is a grand tapestry woven from the threads of fundamental particles, complex systems, and emergent phenomena. From the tiniest atom to the vast complexity of the human brain, nature has achieved a level of sophistication and elegance that science and technology strive to replicate. This chapter explores the profound journey of understanding and replicating nature's most intricate systems-atoms and brains-and the insights they offer into the nature of reality, intelligence, and creation.

The Atom-A Quantum Enigma

Understanding the Atom

The atom, once thought to be the smallest indivisible unit of matter, is now understood as a complex system of protons, neutrons, and electrons governed by the laws of quantum mechanics. Our understanding of the atom spans multiple levels:

Structural: The nucleus and electron orbitals.

Functional: Chemical bonds and periodic trends.

Quantum: Wave-particle duality, superposition, and entanglement.

Can We Replicate an Atom?

While we can simulate and mimic some aspects of atomic behavior, fully replicating an atom at the quantum level remains a challenge. Key efforts include:

Synthetic Atoms: Quantum dots and Rydberg atoms mimic atomic properties.

Quantum Simulations: Quantum computers simulate small molecules like lithium hydride.

Limitations: Quantum complexity, scale, and stability hinder full replication.

Philosophical Implications

Replicating an atom raises questions about the nature of reality:

Wave-Particle Duality: What is an electron "really"?

Emergent Phenomena: How do atoms give rise to complex systems like life and consciousness?

Ethical Considerations: What are the implications of controlling matter at the atomic level?

The Brain-A Biological Masterpiece

Understanding the Brain

The human brain is a marvel of evolution, capable of attention, plasticity, low energy consumption, and emotional intelligence. Its architecture is hierarchical, modular, and distributed, enabling it to integrate diverse functionalities into a unified system.

Can We Replicate the Brain?

Replicating the brain involves understanding and mimicking its subsystems and interactions:

Biological Replication: Brain organoids and synthetic neurons mimic some aspects of brain function.

Computational Replication: Neuromorphic computing and whole-brain simulations aim to replicate brain architecture and behavior.

Challenges: Scale, plasticity, and emergent properties like consciousness remain hurdles.

Philosophical Implications

Creating a biological or computational replica of the brain raises profound questions:

Consciousness: Would a replica be conscious?

Identity: Would it have its own identity or be a copy of the original?

Rights: Should a conscious replica have rights similar to humans?

The Common Thread-Emergence and Complexity

Emergent Properties

Both atoms and brains exhibit emergent properties that arise from the interactions of their components:

Atoms: Chemical bonds and material properties emerge from quantum interactions.

Brains: Consciousness and emotions emerge from neural interactions.

The Role of Architecture

The architecture of atoms and brains enables their functionality:

Atoms: Quantum mechanics governs the behavior of particles.

Brains: Hierarchical, modular, and distributed processing enables complex tasks.

The Role of Fundamental Components

The properties of fundamental components-electrons and neurons-enable the functionality of atoms and brains:

Atoms: Electrons and their quantum behavior.

Brains: Neurons and their plasticity.

The Future of Replication

Replicating Atoms

Advances in quantum computing, synthetic biology, and materials science may bring us closer to replicating atoms:

Quantum Simulations: Simulating larger and more complex systems.

Synthetic Atoms: Creating new forms of matter with unique properties.

Replicating Brains

Advances in neuroscience, AI, and biotechnology may enable us to replicate brain function:

Neuromorphic Computing: Energy-efficient hardware for brain-like computation.

Brain Organoids: Lab-grown brain tissue for studying and replicating brain function.

Ethical and Philosophical Considerations

The ability to replicate atoms and brains raises ethical and philosophical questions:

Control Over Matter: What are the implications of controlling matter at the atomic level?

Consciousness: What does it mean to create a conscious entity?

The Symphony of Creation

The Interconnectedness of All Things

Atoms and brains are not isolated systems but part of a larger, interconnected universe. Understanding and replicating them requires a holistic approach that considers their interactions with the environment and each other.

The Role of Science and Technology

Science and technology are the tools we use to unravel the mysteries of nature. From quantum mechanics to neuroscience, each discovery brings us closer to understanding and replicating the universe's most intricate systems.

The Journey Ahead

The quest to replicate atoms and brains is not just a scientific endeavor but a philosophical and ethical journey. It challenges us to rethink our place in the universe and our responsibilities as creators.

Conclusion: The Symphony of Creation

The universe is a symphony of creation, with atoms and brains as its most intricate notes. Understanding and replicating these systems is a journey that transcends science and technology, touching on the very nature of reality, intelligence, and existence. As we continue to explore the mysteries of atoms and brains, we move closer to unlocking the secrets of the universe and our place within it. The symphony of creation is far from over, and each discovery brings us closer to harmonizing with the cosmos.

This expanded document delves deeper into the complexities of atoms and brains, exploring the quantum realm, neural networks, and the future of replication. It also addresses the ethical and philosophical considerations of creating synthetic entities and the interconnectedness of all things. The narrative weaves together scientific insights, technological advancements, and philosophical reflections, offering a comprehensive and compelling exploration of the symphony of creation.

The ethical development and deployment of artificial cognition require a balance between innovation and regulation, guided by ethical frameworks that address the moral responsibilities and potential risks associated with creating machines with cognitive abilities

CHAPTER 9-THE FRACTAL FLAWS OF HUMAN SYSTEMS

Humanity's greatest strength-our ability to abstract, conceptualize, and build complex systems-is also the source of our greatest vulnerabilities. From the tools we wield to the societies we inhabit; every human creation is a system built on layers of abstraction. These systems, like biological organisms, are prone to errors. In biology, errors occur during gene translation, leading to mutations that shape evolution. In human systems, errors arise during the flow of information-encoding, transmitting, and decoding abstract ideas into tangible structures.

The higher the level of abstraction, the greater the scale and impact of these errors. Human abstraction-our ability to conceptualize ideas like "money," "justice," or "algorithms"-acts as the unit of system design. Each layer of abstraction introduces new error points, and the flaws in these systems are not random but graded by the frequency and severity of information-processing errors.

This chapter explores the fractal nature of flaws in human systems, examining how errors propagate through tools, societies, economies, businesses, and ethical frameworks. By understanding the mechanics of these errors, we can design systems that are more resilient, adaptive, and aligned with human well-being.

1. The Error-Graded Nature of Systems

1.1 Biological vs. Human Systems: A Fractal Analogy

Biological systems and human systems share a fractal nature in their error propagation:

Biological Systems: Errors occur during gene transcription (e.g., DNA replication mistakes), leading to mutations. These errors are localized but propagate through generations, shaping evolution.

Human Systems: Errors arise during the translation of abstract ideas into tangible structures. For example:

Tools: Miscommunication between designers and users leads to inefficient or unsafe designs (e.g., software bugs in self-driving cars)1.

Economies: Flawed assumptions in economic models (e.g., the 2008 financial crisis due to mispriced risk abstractions)1.

Morality: Ethical frameworks fail when abstract principles clash with real-world complexity (e.g., rigid laws causing unintended injustice)1.

Key Insight: Human abstraction-our ability to conceptualize ideas-acts as the unit of system design. Each layer of abstraction introduces new error points, and the complexity of human cognition amplifies these flaws.

The Mechanics of Systemic Errors

Error Propagation in Information Flow

Human systems process information through three stages:

Encoding: Translating abstract ideas into rules (e.g., laws, software code)1.

Transmission: Distributing rules through institutions (e.g., education, markets)1.

Decoding: Individuals interpreting rules (e.g., cultural norms, consumer behavior)1.

Flaws emerge at each stage:

Encoding Errors: Biased assumptions (e.g., GDP as a measure of progress ignores environmental costs)1.

Transmission Errors: Corruption, misinformation, or loss of context (e.g., religious doctrines distorted over centuries)1.

Decoding Errors: Misinterpretation due to cultural or cognitive biases (e.g., algorithmic hiring tools reinforcing gender stereotypes)1.

Example: Social media platforms encode the abstraction of "engagement," transmit it via recommendation algorithms, and users decode it as polarized echo chambers.

Grading Flaws: From Minor Bugs to Existential Risks

The Error Hierarchy

Flaws in human systems can be graded by their scale and impact:

Grade 1 (Minor): Localized inefficiencies (e.g., bureaucratic red tape slowing innovation)1.

Grade 2 (Structural): Systemic inequalities (e.g., wealth gaps from tax policies favoring capital over labor)1.

Grade 3 (Critical): Cascading failures (e.g., climate inaction due to short-term economic abstractions)1.

Case Study:

Tools: The Boeing 737 MAX crashes resulted from encoding errors (faulty sensor logic) and transmission errors (regulatory failures)1.

Ethics: Utilitarianism fails when abstract "greater good" calculations ignore individual rights (e.g., unethical medical trials)1.

The Role of Abstraction in Amplifying Errors

Abstraction as a Double-Edged Sword

Human abstraction enables complex systems but multiplies error risks:

Positive Feedback: Higher abstraction allows innovation (e.g., blockchain, democratic governance)1.

Negative Feedback: Errors compound as systems grow detached from physical reality (e.g., speculative financial derivatives)1.

Example:

Money: A foundational abstraction. Errors in its design (e.g., fiat currency inflation) or transmission (e.g., hyperinflation in Zimbabwe) destabilize societies.

Cognitive Tools: The Source and Solution

The Brain's Error-Prone Abstraction Engine

Human cognition-the origin of abstraction-is itself flawed:

Heuristics: Mental shortcuts (e.g., "growth = progress") lead to systemic blind spots.

Metacognition: Tools like science and philosophy mitigate errors by formalizing doubt (e.g., peer review, ethical audits)1.

Example:

Scientific Method: Reduces encoding errors via falsifiability but struggles with transmission (e.g., politicization of climate science)1.

Evolutionary Paths: Error Correction vs. Entropy

Adaptive vs. Maladaptive Systems

Systems evolve by balancing error correction with innovation:

Biological Analogy: Natural selection eliminates harmful mutations.

Human Systems:

Adaptive: Open-source software (continuous bug fixes via decentralized input)1.

Maladaptive: Authoritarian regimes (suppressing error feedback until collapse)1.

Future Trajectories:

Tools: AI systems that self-audit for biases (reducing decoding errors)1.

Economies: Doughnut economics (encoding ecological limits into growth models)1.

The Ethical Imperative: Minimizing Harm in an Error-Ridden World

Error-Aware Design

To mitigate flaws, systems must:

Acknowledge Abstraction Limits: No model fully captures reality.

Build Feedback Loops: Democratize error detection (e.g., citizen assemblies for policy testing)1.

Prioritize Resilience Over Efficiency: Systems that tolerate small errors avoid catastrophic ones (e.g., decentralized energy grids)1.

Example:

Ethical AI: Encoding fairness constraints, transmitting transparency, and decoding with human oversight.

Future Implications: Navigating the Path Ahead

Technological Advancements and Their Impact

As technology continues to advance, the complexity of human systems will increase, introducing new layers of abstraction and potential errors. Innovations in artificial intelligence, quantum computing, and biotechnology will transform how we live and work, but they will also pose new ethical and practical challenges. Ensuring that these technologies are developed and deployed responsibly will be crucial for minimizing harm and maximizing benefits.

Societal and Economic Shifts

The future will see significant shifts in societal and economic structures. Globalization, demographic changes, and environmental pressures will reshape economies and societies. Adapting to these changes will require flexible and resilient systems that can learn from errors and evolve in response to new challenges. Policies that promote inclusivity, sustainability, and equity will be essential for creating stable and prosperous societies.

Ethical Considerations and Governance

Ethical considerations will play a central role in shaping the future of human systems. As we navigate the complexities of emerging technologies and global challenges, ethical frameworks will need to evolve to address new dilemmas. Transparent and inclusive governance structures will be necessary to ensure that decisions are made in the best interest of humanity as a whole.

The Role of Education and Lifelong Learning

Education will be a key driver of future progress. Equipping individuals with the skills and knowledge needed to navigate complex systems and adapt to change will be essential. Lifelong learning will become increasingly important as the pace of technological and societal change accelerates. Educational institutions will need to innovate and collaborate with industry and government to provide relevant and accessible learning opportunities.

Conclusion

Human systems are fractal networks of abstraction, where errors in information processing determine their flaws. Unlike biological systems, our capacity for abstract thought amplifies both creativity and risk. By grading errors-from misaligned incentives to existential threats-we can design systems that harness abstraction's power while hedging against its pitfalls.

The challenge is not to eliminate errors but to build structures that learn from them, ensuring our creations evolve with humanity, not against it. In an age of increasing complexity, the systems that thrive will be those that embrace their flaws, adapt to feedback, and align with the deeper truths of human existence.

Key Takeaways:

Abstraction is the unit of human systems, and errors in information flow are the root of systemic flaws.

Flaws are graded by their scale and impact, from minor inefficiencies to existential risks.

Error-aware design-through feedback loops, resilience, and ethical oversight-can mitigate the risks of abstraction.

The future of human systems lies in balancing innovation with error correction, ensuring they evolve in harmony with humanity's needs.

This chapter invites us to see our creations not as perfect machines but as evolving organisms, shaped by the interplay of abstraction, error, and adaptation. By embracing this perspective, we can build a world that is not only smarter but also wiser.

The integration of artificial cognition into the workforce will transform industries by automating tasks, displacing some jobs, and creating new opportunities, necessitating reskilling and education to prepare the workforce for a future where humans and machines collaborate

CHAPTER 10-THE HUMAN BRAIN – A BLUEPRINT FOR FUTURE AI SYSTEMS

The human brain is not just an organ; it is a testament to the power of evolution, a masterpiece of biological engineering that has been refined over millions of years. It is the seat of our thoughts, emotions, creativity, and consciousness-a system so complex and efficient that it continues to baffle scientists and inspire technologists. What makes the brain truly remarkable is not just its ability to process information but the principles that underpin its functionality: adaptability, efficiency, and the seamless integration of diverse processes. These principles are not only the foundation of human intelligence but also a treasure trove of insights for the future of artificial intelligence (AI).

This chapter explores the brain's core functionalities, not merely as isolated facts but as interconnected systems that work in harmony to create intelligence. By delving into these principles, we can uncover profound insights into how the brain achieves its extraordinary capabilities and how these insights can guide the development of AI systems that are not just intelligent but also adaptive, efficient, and human-like. The chapter concludes with a reflection on the challenges and ethical implications of replicating the brain, whether biologically or computationally, and what it means for the future of AI and humanity.

Attention and Focus: The Brain's Selective Filter

Insights into Functionality

The brain's ability to focus on relevant information while filtering out distractions is not just a mechanical process; it is a dynamic interplay of prioritization and context-awareness. Attention is not static-it shifts based on goals, emotions, and environmental cues. This adaptability allows the brain to allocate resources efficiently, ensuring that critical tasks receive the necessary cognitive bandwidth.

Implications for AI

While AI systems like transformer models have made strides in mimicking attention through self-attention mechanisms, they lack the brain's fluidity. The brain's attention system is deeply integrated with memory, emotion, and context, enabling it to prioritize tasks dynamically. Future AI systems could benefit from incorporating similar integrative mechanisms, allowing them to adapt their focus based on real-time needs and environmental changes.

Plasticity and Adaptability: The Brain's Learning Power

Insights into Functionality

Plasticity is the brain's superpower. It is not just about rewiring neurons; it is about the brain's ability to evolve continuously. From learning a new skill to recovering from injury, plasticity ensures that the brain remains a lifelong learner. This adaptability is rooted in the brain's ability to balance stability and change-preserving essential knowledge while integrating new information.

Implications for AI

Current AI systems struggle with catastrophic forgetting, where learning new tasks erases previous knowledge. The brain's plasticity offers a blueprint for overcoming this challenge. By developing AI systems that can dynamically adjust their architecture and retain critical information, we can create machines that learn and adapt over time, much like humans.

Energy Efficiency and Sparse Coding: The Brain's Optimization

Insights into Functionality

The brain's energy efficiency is a marvel of nature. Operating on just ~20 watts, it outperforms even the most advanced supercomputers. This efficiency is achieved through sparse coding, where only a small fraction of neurons are active at any given time. This selective activation not only conserves energy but also reduces noise, ensuring precise and reliable information processing.

Implications for AI

AI systems, particularly large-scale models, are notoriously energy-intensive. By adopting the brain's principles of sparse coding and energy-efficient communication, we can design AI systems that are both powerful and sustainable. Neuromorphic hardware, which mimics the brain's architecture, is a promising step in this direction.

Parallel, Distributed, and Hierarchical Processing: The Brain's Multitasking Mastery

Insights into Functionality

The brain's ability to process information in parallel across billions of neurons is a key factor in its efficiency. This distributed processing is complemented by a hierarchical structure, where information flows from low-level sensory inputs to high-level abstract reasoning. This combination allows the brain to handle multiple tasks simultaneously while maintaining coherence and context.

Implications for AI

While AI systems like deep learning models use hierarchical layers for feature extraction, they often lack the brain's seamless integration of parallel and distributed processing. Future AI systems could benefit from architectures that combine hierarchical processing with distributed computation, enabling them to handle complex, real-world tasks more effectively.

Feedback Loops and Predictive Coding: The Brain's Error Correction

Insights into Functionality

The brain is not just reactive; it is predictive. It constantly generates models of the world and updates them based on feedback. This predictive coding minimizes errors and refines behavior, ensuring that actions are aligned with goals. Feedback loops are integral to this process, allowing the brain to learn from mistakes and adapt to new information.

Implications for AI

AI systems often struggle with real-time adaptation and error correction. By incorporating predictive coding and feedback loops, we can create AI systems that are more resilient and capable of learning from experience. This would enable machines to refine their actions dynamically, much like the brain.

Redundancy, Fault Tolerance, and Robustness: The Brain's Resilience

Insights into Functionality

The brain's resilience lies in its redundancy and fault tolerance. Multiple neural pathways can perform the same function, ensuring that the brain remains functional even when parts of it are damaged. This redundancy is complemented by the brain's ability to filter out noise and focus on relevant information, making it robust in chaotic environments.

Implications for AI

AI systems are often brittle, failing catastrophically when faced with unexpected inputs or errors. By incorporating redundancy and fault tolerance into AI architectures, we can create systems that are more robust and reliable. This would make AI more adaptable to real-world conditions, where noise and uncertainty are inevitable.

Contextual Understanding and Emotional Intelligence: The Brain's Nuanced Processing

Insights into Functionality

The brain's ability to understand context and integrate emotions into decision-making is what sets it apart from machines. Contextual understanding allows the brain to interpret information in a nuanced way, while emotional intelligence enables it to navigate social interactions and make decisions that align with goals and values.

Implications for AI

Current AI systems lack the brain's ability to understand context and emotions. By developing models that integrate contextual awareness and emotional intelligence, we can create AI systems that are more human-like in their interactions and decision-making. This would enable machines to operate effectively in complex, real-world environments.

Generalization, Abstraction, and Intrinsic Motivation: The Brain's Creative Drive

Insights into Functionality

The brain's ability to generalize from limited examples and think abstractly is the foundation of creativity and problem-solving. This is driven by intrinsic motivation-the brain's innate curiosity and desire to explore. These qualities enable the brain to learn, innovate, and adapt in ways that go beyond mere data processing.

Implications for AI

AI systems often struggle with generalization and abstraction, relying on vast amounts of data to perform tasks. By incorporating principles of intrinsic motivation and meta-learning, we can create AI systems that learn more efficiently and creatively. This would enable machines to tackle novel problems and generate innovative solutions.

Temporal Processing and Self-Organization: The Brain's Mastery of Time and Order

Insights into Functionality

The brain's ability to process time-varying information, such as speech and movement, is a testament to its mastery of temporal dynamics. This is complemented by its capacity for self-organization, where neural circuits adapt and organize themselves based on input patterns and learning experiences.

Implications for AI

AI systems often struggle with temporal processing and self-organization. By developing models that better capture temporal dynamics and self-organizing principles, we can create AI systems that are more adaptive and capable of handling real-time tasks. This would enable machines to operate more effectively in dynamic environments.

Consciousness and Self-Awareness: The Ultimate Frontier

Insights into Functionality

Consciousness and self-awareness are the most enigmatic aspects of the brain. They represent the pinnacle of its functionality, enabling introspection, subjective experience, and a sense of identity. While the mechanisms behind consciousness remain poorly understood, theories like global workspace theory and integrated information theory offer intriguing possibilities.

Implications for AI

The quest for artificial consciousness is both exciting and fraught with ethical challenges. While replicating consciousness in machines remains a distant goal, exploring frameworks for artificial consciousness could lead to breakthroughs in our understanding of both the brain and AI. However, this endeavor must be approached with caution, as it raises profound questions about identity, rights, and the nature of consciousness itself.

Replicating the Human Brain: Organic vs. Inorganic Systems

Replicating with Alternative Organic Materials

The idea of replicating the human brain using alternative organic materials, such as synthetic neurons or bioengineered tissues, is an intriguing possibility. Organic materials could potentially mimic the brain's biological properties more closely, including its plasticity, energy efficiency, and ability to self-organize. Advances in synthetic biology and brain organoids are already paving the way for such innovations.

Challenges and Possibilities

Complexity: Replicating the brain's ~86 billion neurons and ~100 trillion synapses with organic materials is a monumental task.

Dynamic Nature: Organic systems are inherently dynamic and adaptable, but controlling and replicating these properties artificially is challenging.

Ethical Concerns: Creating a biological brain raises ethical questions about consciousness, identity, and rights.

Replicating with Inorganic Systems

Inorganic systems, such as silicon-based computers and neuromorphic hardware, offer a more practical and scalable approach to replicating the brain's functionalities. These systems can leverage existing technologies and computational frameworks to mimic the brain's architecture and processes.

Challenges and Possibilities

Energy Efficiency: Inorganic systems are far less energy-efficient than the brain, requiring megawatts of power for large-scale simulations.

Plasticity: Inorganic systems lack the brain's inherent plasticity, making it difficult to replicate its adaptability and learning capabilities.

Emergent Properties: Replicating emergent behaviors like consciousness and emotions in inorganic systems remains a significant challenge.

Computational Architectures for Replicating Brain Functionalities

Beyond Transformers and Deep Networks

While transformer models and deep neural networks have been successful in replicating certain brain functionalities, such as attention and abstraction, they are not the only computational architectures available.

Exploring alternative architectures could provide new insights and capabilities.

Alternative Architectures

Spiking Neural Networks (SNNs): Mimic the brain's spike-based communication, offering energy-efficient and biologically plausible models for temporal processing and learning.

Self-Organizing Maps (SOMs): Unsupervised learning models that can organize and represent data in a way that resembles the brain's self-organization.

Bayesian Networks: Probabilistic models that can handle uncertainty and make predictions, similar to the brain's predictive coding.

Capsule Networks: Designed to capture hierarchical relationships and spatial information, offering a more nuanced approach to feature extraction and abstraction.

Hybrid Models: Combining neural networks with symbolic AI to replicate higher-order reasoning and generalization.

Implications for AI

By exploring and integrating these alternative architectures, we can create AI systems that are more versatile and capable of replicating a wider range of brain functionalities. This would enable machines to handle complex, real-world tasks more effectively and efficiently.

Key Differences Between Biological and Computational Systems

Feature	Biological Brain	Computational Replica
Architecture	Hierarchical, modular, distributed	Hierarchical, modular, distributed
Energy Efficiency	~20 watts	Megawatts for large-scale simulations
Plasticity	High (synaptic plasticity, neurogenesis)	Limited (requires retraining)
Emergent Properties	Consciousness, emotions, creativity	Limited or absent in current models
Scalability	Naturally scalable	Limited by computational resources

The Brain's Information Network: A City Built for Thought

Imagine two cities built from the same set of blueprints, each with thousands of identical building blocks, just as every living organism starts with the same fundamental DNA code. One city, however, has an exquisitely organized network of roads, bridges, and transit hubs that allow its citizens to interact rapidly, share ideas seamlessly, and adapt quickly to new challenges. The other city, despite having the same number of buildings, suffers from a chaotic jumble of poorly connected streets. In this analogy, the buildings are like the neurons in a brain, and the roadways are like the synapses that connect them.

In biological brains, intelligence doesn't depend on the sheer amount of DNA or even the raw count of neurons. Instead, it emerges from the architecture of the brain's neural network—how neurons connect, communicate, and cooperate to process information. Several fundamental components and metrics help us understand the limits and capabilities of cognition:

Neural Network Connectivity and Efficiency:

Global Efficiency: This metric, borrowed from graph theory, measures how quickly information can travel between any two neurons across the entire brain network. A brain with high global efficiency is like a city with an excellent highway system that minimizes travel time, enabling rapid and effective communication across distant regions.

Clustering Coefficient: This measures the degree to which neurons tend to form local cliques or tightly knit groups. Just as neighborhood associations can foster local innovation in a city, high local clustering can support specialized processing and complex computations in the brain.

Small-worldness and Modularity: Many brain networks exhibit a small-world architecture, characterized by dense local clustering combined with short global paths, which strikes an optimal balance between local processing and global integration. Modularity refers to the brain's organization into distinct subnetworks or modules that handle different functions. Efficient modularity allows for both specialized tasks and their coordination, much like specialized districts in a city that are linked by effective transport corridors.

Dynamic Adaptability and Plasticity: Beyond static connectivity, a brain's ability to reconfigure its network through synaptic plasticity is crucial for learning and adaptation. This is akin to a city that can quickly change its traffic patterns in response to new demands, disasters, or opportunities.

White Matter Integrity: Techniques like diffusion tensor imaging (DTI) assess the integrity of the brain's wiring (axon pathways). Just as the condition of roads influences how well traffic flows, the health and coherence of white matter tracts are critical for cognitive speed and efficiency.

Functional Integration Metrics: Information Integration: Measures such as the integration or centrality of nodes (neurons) indicate how pivotal certain regions are in uniting the brain's activity. Regions with high centrality might be seen as major transit hubs in our city analogy—they help coordinate and disseminate information across the network.

Behavioral and Cognitive Metrics: Ultimately, intelligence is also measured by performance on tasks such as IQ tests, reaction times, working memory capacity, and problem-solving skills. These behavioral measures are the output of the brain's network. Researchers then correlate these outputs with neuroimaging metrics to understand how neural network properties underlie cognitive performance.

Consider a young inventor in a bustling metropolis. Her ideas and innovations aren't determined merely by the number of tools in her workshop, the equivalent of the raw DNA code, but by how she organizes those tools, how effectively she can switch between different projects, and how swiftly she can integrate new information into her designs. Similarly, two individuals might share a nearly identical genetic blueprint, yet one develops exceptional problem-solving abilities because her brain's neural network is wired with optimal connectivity, high efficiency, and dynamic adaptability.

In scientific research, advanced neuroimaging techniques like functional MRI (fMRI) and diffusion tensor imaging (DTI) act as our aerial photographs and traffic sensors, revealing how effectively the brain's city is connected. Researchers calculate metrics such as global efficiency, clustering coefficient, and modularity to quantify these properties, much as urban planners might evaluate the quality of a city's infrastructure.

Thus, while the DNA blueprint sets the stage, it is the emergent properties of the neural network—the organization, connectivity, and efficiency—that truly define the limits and capabilities of intelligence and cognition in living organisms. This perspective underscores why simply having more DNA or more neurons doesn't automatically yield greater intelligence. It's all about the quality and organization of the connections, the city planning of the brain, that ultimately shapes our cognitive abilities.

In Summary:

Intelligence Is More Than DNA or Neuron Count: Like a city, it depends on the quality of its connections, the efficiency of its transit systems, and the flexibility of its design.

Key Metrics Include: Neuron count, synaptic connectivity, firing rate, conduction speed, global efficiency, and clustering/modularity—all of which can be combined in a theoretical framework.

Calculating a Theoretical Limit: One can estimate an upper bound on individual intelligence by modeling the brain as an information-processing network and calculating its maximum integrated processing capacity. Although highly theoretical, this approach uses the brain's structure and function as a proxy for the limits of cognitive ability.

Real-World Relevance: While this limit is a theoretical construct—subject to biological constraints and dynamic learning—it highlights the idea that true intelligence is an emergent property of complex, efficient, and adaptable neural networks rather than simply a matter of more DNA or more neurons.

This conceptual roadmap bridges the biological city planning of the brain with the mathematical tools of information theory and network analysis, suggesting one way that we might begin to calculate a theoretical measurement of the limit of individual intelligence.

Conclusion: Toward Human-Like AI

The human brain is more than a collection of functionalities; it is a symphony of interconnected systems that work in harmony to create intelligence. By studying these systems, we gain not just facts but profound insights into what makes the brain so extraordinary. These insights offer a roadmap for the future of AI, guiding us toward systems that are not just intelligent but also adaptive, efficient, and human-like.

However, the journey to replicating the brain, whether biologically or computationally, is fraught with challenges. From scalability and energy efficiency to the ethical implications of creating conscious machines, the road ahead is complex and uncertain. Yet, the potential rewards are immense. By unlocking the secrets of the brain, we can create AI systems that enhance our lives, solve complex problems, and perhaps even help us understand ourselves better.

This journey is not just a scientific endeavor; it is a profound exploration of what it means to be human. As we continue to push the boundaries of AI, we must do so with humility, curiosity, and a deep respect for the mysteries of the brain. For in understanding the brain, we may ultimately come to understand ourselves.

HUMAN-MACHINE COLLABORATION,
WHERE HUMAN CREATIVITY AND MACHINE
EFFICIENCY COMBINE, ENHANCES
OUTCOMES ACROSS VARIOUS DOMAINS BY
DESIGNING INTERFACES AND SYSTEMS
THAT OPTIMIZE HUMAN-MACHINE
INTERACTION

CHAPTER 11- AI and Theory of MIND

Artificial Intelligence (AI) has made significant strides in recent years, but one area where it continues to evolve is in its ability to understand and respond to human emotions, intentions, and beliefs-an ability referred to as Theory of Mind (ToM). This chapter explores what ToM is, how it's being integrated into AI, and its potential real-world applications across diverse sectors such as healthcare, social robotics, education, content moderation, and more.

Understanding Theory of Mind

Theory of Mind (ToM) is a cognitive ability to attribute mental states-such as beliefs, desires, intentions, and emotions-to oneself and others. It also involves understanding that others have thoughts and perspectives different from one's own. This ability is essential for social interaction, empathy, and predicting others' behavior.

Components of Theory of Mind

Understanding Mental States: Recognizing that people have thoughts, beliefs, and emotions, and that these states influence how individuals act.

False Beliefs: Realizing that someone can hold a belief about the world that is not true. For example, a child knows a toy is hidden in a closet but understands that their friend, who didn't see the hiding, believes it's in the toybox.

Second-Order Thinking: Thinking about what someone else believes about a third person's belief or perspective. For example, "John thinks that Mary believes the book is on the table."

Interpretive Understanding: Recognizing that people interpret ambiguous information differently. For example, seeing an abstract painting as a duck versus a rabbit.

Emotional ToM: Understanding others' emotions and how they change based on events or situations. For example, predicting happiness, sadness, or surprise in another person.

Advanced ToM (Deception and Sarcasm): Detecting when someone is being sarcastic, ironic, or deceptive. For example, interpreting "Nice job" as genuine or sarcastic based on context.

Origins of ToM Research

ToM begins developing around 18 months with rudimentary forms like recognizing intentions. By 4–5 years, children typically pass "false belief tasks," a hallmark of ToM. Advanced ToM (sarcasm, irony, layered thinking) develops into adolescence and beyond. Research has also explored whether animals, such as chimpanzees, have a form of ToM. They often exhibit behaviors suggesting basic ToM abilities, like recognizing others' intentions.

How ToM Benchmarks Are Created

To evaluate Theory of Mind in humans or AI, researchers use tasks designed to test specific components of ToM. These benchmarks often simulate real-life scenarios that require reasoning about mental states.

False Belief Tasks (First-Order and Second-Order): Classic test: Sally-Anne Task. Sally places a marble in a basket and leaves. Anne moves the marble to a box. Where will Sally look for the marble? This task tests whether the subject understands that Sally holds a belief different from reality.

Smarties Task: A child is shown a box labeled "Smarties" (a candy) that contains pencils. When asked what another person would think is in the box, success demonstrates an understanding of false beliefs.

Second-Order Beliefs: Testing nested reasoning: "What does John think that Sarah believes?"

Interpretive Tasks: Example: A story or image with ambiguous meaning. Subjects are asked to explain how different individuals interpret it.

Deception Tasks: Subjects assess whether a statement or action was intended to deceive.

Emotional Understanding: Inferring how a character feels in a given situation based on context (e.g., losing a toy but finding a new one).

Sarcasm/Irony: Detecting non-literal language or sarcasm in dialogue.

Designing Benchmarks for AI ToM

To test AI's ToM abilities, benchmarks are designed similarly to human tasks but adapted for language and logic comprehension.

Challenges in AI Benchmarks

Literal Thinking: AI often struggles with ambiguity, sarcasm, or layered beliefs.

World Knowledge: Unlike humans, AI lacks real-world experiences and relies on training data.

Context Awareness: Complex ToM tasks require maintaining context over multiple exchanges, which can be challenging for AI.

ToM Benchmarks for AI

Benchmarks such as ToMi (Theory of Mind in AI) use structured datasets of scenarios covering multiple levels of ToM tasks. Scenarios often include first-order beliefs, second-order beliefs, and deception detection.

Creating ToM Benchmarks for AI

Scenario Selection: Use real-world-inspired or controlled experimental scenarios. Ensure diversity across cultures and contexts.

Gradual Complexity: Start with basic tasks like false beliefs and progress to advanced reasoning (e.g., sarcasm detection).

Metrics: Accuracy: Whether the AI's answer matches human expectations. Consistency: Repeatability of correct answers. Response Time: Time taken to infer mental states.

Human Baseline: Test scenarios on humans (adults and children) to set benchmarks.

Comparison: Compare AI's performance against human baselines and across different AI models.

Interpreting Results in AI ToM Tasks

Performance Metrics

Accuracy: If AI performs well on first-order tasks (~95%), it may have basic ToM abilities. Lower performance on second-order or sarcasm tasks reveals limitations.

Error Analysis: Literal misunderstandings (e.g., failing sarcasm). Incorrect attributions of beliefs or intentions.

Response Time: AI is typically faster than humans, but reasoning speed should not compromise accuracy.

Comparative Analysis

Compare different AI models (e.g., GPT-4 vs. LLaMA 3.2) on accuracy across ToM levels, ability to handle nuanced reasoning (sarcasm, deception), consistency, and error rates.

Insights

Strengths: AI excels in structured reasoning tasks (e.g., basic false beliefs).

Weaknesses: Struggles with subtle emotional reasoning, ambiguity, and cultural nuances.

Applications of ToM in AI

Here are several practical applications of ToM in AI systems that enhance human-AI interactions across industries:

Social Robotics: Human-Robot Interaction

Objective: Enable robots to understand and interact naturally with humans by recognizing emotions, beliefs, and intentions.

Use Case: Social Assistants and Elderly Care Robots

AI-driven robots in healthcare settings can use ToM to predict emotional states and adapt their responses. For example, a robot may identify if an elderly person is anxious about being alone and offer reassurance or suggest a call to a loved one. Similarly, if a robot detects frustration over medication management, it might gently suggest assistance.

How ToM Helps: Emotion Recognition: The robot can infer emotions based on tone, facial expressions, or physical cues and respond accordingly. Need Prediction: Anticipating needs based on past behavior, like suggesting activities if the person shows signs of boredom or depression.

Mental Health and Therapy: AI as a Therapeutic Companion

Objective: Create AI systems that can provide mental health support by understanding and responding to a user's emotions and mental state.

Use Case: Virtual Therapy Assistants

An AI-powered chatbot or virtual assistant can use ToM to detect shifts in a user's emotional state and provide appropriate responses, such as offering validation, coping mechanisms, or suggesting professional help when needed.

How ToM Helps: Emotion and Belief Understanding: AI can recognize frustration or sadness in a person's text or speech and respond empathetically, helping individuals feel heard. Contextual Awareness: The AI can track emotional journeys, offering personalized responses based on the user's previous statements.

Example: A user may express feelings of isolation, and the AI responds: "It sounds like you're feeling alone right now. Sometimes reaching out to a friend can help. Would you like help with that?"

Personalized Education: Adaptive Learning with Emotional Awareness

Objective: Empower AI tutors to provide personalized learning experiences that take into account a student's emotional and cognitive state.

Use Case: AI Tutors in Education

In an online learning platform, AI can detect frustration when a student struggles with a problem. By adjusting the difficulty of tasks or offering additional explanations, the AI can help the student move past roadblocks without overwhelming them.

How ToM Helps: Recognizing Cognitive Overload: When students express confusion, the AI can offer simpler tasks or break complex topics into smaller steps. Emotional Sensitivity: Detecting frustration or excitement and adjusting feedback tone accordingly.

Example: An AI tutor notices a student is stuck on a math problem. It can say, "I noticed you've been working on this for a while. Let me explain it in a different way to make it easier."

Content Moderation and Online Communication: Detecting Harmful Behavior

Objective: Enhance AI's ability to understand subtle human interactions, such as sarcasm or emotional manipulation, in online content.

Use Case: Social Media Monitoring

AI systems can detect not only harmful language like hate speech but also subtle, indirect communication like sarcasm, passive-aggressive comments, or deceptive posts. This helps social platforms moderate content effectively and promote a safer online environment.

How ToM Helps: Sarcasm Detection: AI can understand when a statement meant to be sarcastic could be harmful or misleading. Emotion Analysis: Detecting tone and emotional cues to flag inappropriate or manipulative content.

Example: A post that sarcastically says, "Great job, I'm sure that'll solve everything" could be flagged as inappropriate if it's clearly mocking or belittling someone.

Human-AI Collaboration in Creative Tasks

Objective: Enable AI to assist in creative processes by understanding a user's preferences, style, and emotional context.

Use Case: Co-Creating Stories and Art

AI can assist writers, artists, and musicians by providing suggestions that align with their creative intentions. For instance, an AI writing assistant can recommend plot twists based on the emotional tone of the existing narrative.

How ToM Helps: Creative Intent Understanding: The AI can suggest ideas that align with the writer's emotional tone and narrative style. Empathy in Creativity: Understanding the emotional journey the user wants to convey through their work and assisting them accordingly.

Example: A user writing a sad story may get suggestions for melancholic plot twists or emotionally charged dialogues to enhance the tone.

Conclusion: The Future of AI with Theory of Mind

Incorporating Theory of Mind into AI allows for more sophisticated, human-like interactions. AI systems equipped with ToM can better understand and predict human behavior, leading to more personalized, empathetic, and effective outcomes. From social robots and mental health assistants to autonomous vehicles and e-commerce platforms, ToM is set to revolutionize the way we interact with machines.

As AI continues to advance, the integration of ToM will not only improve AI's technical abilities but also enhance the emotional and social intelligence required to navigate the complexities of human behavior.

Artificial cognition has inherent limits in replicating human-like understanding, creativity, and emotional intelligence, and overestimating its capabilities poses significant risks

CHAPTER 12-INTEGRATED INFORMATION THEORY (IIT)

Integrated Information Theory (IIT) is one of the most intriguing scientific approaches to understanding consciousness-the subjective experience of being aware. Developed by neuroscientist Giulio Tononi, IIT offers a mathematical and conceptual framework to explain why certain physical systems (like the brain) generate consciousness while others (like a computer or a rock) do not.

In this chapter, we'll explore the foundations of IIT, its key principles, how it measures consciousness, its potential applications, the importance of IIT, how it compares to alternative theories of consciousness, and how it is being integrated into artificial intelligence (AI).

What is Integrated Information Theory?

At its core, IIT proposes that consciousness arises from the way information is integrated in a system. According to IIT, any system with a high degree of integrated information has some level of consciousness. The theory attempts to answer two fundamental questions:

1.   Why does consciousness exist?

2.   What physical systems are capable of having subjective experiences?

The Central Concept: (Phi)

The hallmark of IIT is the quantification of integrated information, represented by. This value measures how much information a system generates as a whole, beyond the information generated by its individual parts. High indicates that a system's components work together in a unified, interdependent manner, making it conscious.

The Importance of IIT: Why Was It Developed?

1. Addressing the Hard Problem of Consciousness

The "hard problem of consciousness," a term coined by philosopher David Chalmers, refers to the difficulty of explaining why and how physical processes in the brain give rise to subjective experiences (qualia). IIT was developed to bridge this gap by providing a quantitative framework for understanding how consciousness emerges from physical systems.

2. Bridging Subjective Experience and Physical Systems

Traditional neuroscience focuses on mapping brain activity to behavior, but it doesn't explain how or why these processes feel like anything from the first-person perspective. IIT seeks to connect the subjective and the objective by identifying the physical properties that correspond to consciousness.

3. Clinical Applications

IIT offers potential tools for diagnosing and understanding disorders of consciousness, such as:

- Coma and vegetative states: By measuring , clinicians may better differentiate between patients with varying levels of awareness.

- Locked-in syndrome: IIT can help identify conscious patients who are unable to communicate through traditional means.

4. Defining Consciousness in Artificial Intelligence

As AI systems become increasingly sophisticated, questions arise about whether they can be conscious. IIT provides a rigorous way to assess whether a system has the integrated information necessary for consciousness. It emphasizes that consciousness is not merely about complex behavior but about the structural integration of information.

5. Ethical Implications

Understanding what systems are conscious has profound ethical implications, including:

- Treatment of non-human animals.

- The ethical use of AI systems.

- End-of-life care for patients in altered states of consciousness.

Alternative Theories of Consciousness

While IIT is a leading framework, other theories propose alternative explanations for the nature and origin of consciousness. Each theory emphasizes different aspects of the phenomenon:

1. Global Workspace Theory (GWT)

- Proposed by: Bernard Baars.

- Core Idea: Consciousness arises from the brain broadcasting information to a "global workspace," enabling it to be shared across different cognitive processes.

- Focus: Functional integration and working memory.

2. Higher-Order Thought (HOT) Theory

- Proposed by: David Rosenthal and others.

- Core Idea: A mental state becomes conscious when it is accompanied by a higher-order thought about that state (a thought about a thought).

- Focus: Self-awareness and meta-cognition.

3. Predictive Processing and Free Energy Principle

- Proposed by: Karl Friston and others.

- Core Idea: Consciousness arises as the brain minimizes prediction errors by generating models of the world and updating them with sensory input.

- Focus: Predictive coding and active inference.

4. Panpsychism

- Proposed by: Philosophers such as Philip Goff and Galen Strawson.

- Core Idea: Consciousness is a fundamental property of the universe, present to some degree in all physical systems.

5. Recurrent Processing Theory (RPT)

- Proposed by: Victor Lamme.

- Core Idea: Consciousness arises from recurrent (feedback) interactions between brain regions, particularly in sensory processing.

Integrating IIT into Artificial Intelligence

1. Graph-Based Neural Networks

IIT-inspired AI often uses graph-based architectures where nodes represent computational units (e.g., artificial neurons) and edges represent causal relationships. This approach helps simulate integrated information by allowing nodes to interact in complex, interdependent ways.

• Example: Researchers are developing graph neural networks (GNNs) with feedback loops, enabling systems to exhibit high interdependence and integration.

2. Algorithms to Approximate

Measuring in AI systems is computationally intensive, but researchers are working on approximate methods:

• Partition Testing: Dividing an AI model into subsystems and measuring how much information is lost.

• Application: Evaluating whether an AI's internal structure supports high integration.

3. Meta-Cognition in AI

Meta-cognition-the ability to monitor and evaluate one's own processes-is a step toward IIT-inspired architectures.

• Examples:

• AI systems capable of analyzing their decision-making (e.g., explaining why they classified an image in a specific way).

• Models that assess their own performance to improve future learning.

4. Hybrid AI Architectures

Combining symbolic AI (reasoning) with neural networks (pattern recognition) can simulate aspects of IIT:

- Symbolic AI provides explicit causal relationships.

- Neural networks allow for complex state differentiation and integration.

5. Simulating Subjective Experience

Some researchers are building AI systems capable of narrating their internal states, which may simulate basic subjective experiences:

- Example: An AI reporting, "I see a blue circle and feel uncertain about its classification," demonstrates primitive self-awareness.

6. Ethical Considerations

If IIT-inspired AI systems achieve high , questions about their consciousness and rights will arise:

- Should conscious AI have ethical protections?

- How do we validate and verify consciousness in artificial systems?

Conclusion

Integrated Information Theory represents a groundbreaking framework for understanding consciousness, offering insights into neuroscience, philosophy, and artificial intelligence. Its focus on intrinsic integration and differentiation sets it apart from other theories, providing a rigorous, testable model for linking subjective experiences with physical systems.

The integration of IIT into AI holds promise for developing systems that are not only intelligent but potentially conscious. By quantifying , researchers can design AI architectures that emulate integrated information, raising both technical possibilities and profound ethical questions. Whether through meta-cognitive AI, hybrid architectures, or new metrics for consciousness, IIT has the potential to revolutionize our understanding of both natural and artificial minds.

SECTION 3

Beyond the Horizon-Embracing the Dawn of Shared Intelligence: Imagine standing at the edge of a vast, uncharted ocean at sunrise. The sky burns with brilliant hues as the first light of a new day stretches into infinity. In that moment, we sense that beyond the horizon lies a realm of possibilities-dimensions yet unexplored, where the power of collective intelligence awaits to redefine what it means to exist. This is the essence of our next great revolution.

In this chapter, we explore how our evolving shared intelligence, combined with the transformative forces of artificial intelligence (AI), consciousness, and the timeless tools of spirituality, ethics, and morality, is poised to open new dimensions of control over space, time, and our very destiny.

The Evolution of Shared Intelligence

For millennia, human intelligence has been a solitary spark-each individual a unique flame in the darkness. But as our connections deepened, these sparks merged into a radiant blaze of collective understanding. Our societies, cultures, and technologies are all expressions of this shared intelligence-a self-replicating loop where each discovery builds upon the last.

The Journey So Far

From Isolated Minds to Global Networks: Early human communities communicated through oral traditions and art, weaving wisdom into stories passed down through generations. With the invention of writing, printing, and ultimately the digital revolution, our collective intelligence expanded exponentially. Each new medium allowed us to share insights, refine ideas, and transcend the limitations of individual cognition.

The Birth of Artificial Intelligence as an Amplifier: Today, AI stands as our most powerful tool for further integration. Far from merely processing data, AI enables us to interconnect disparate fields of knowledge-merging science with art, economics with ethics, and even logic with spirituality. In doing so, it accelerates our journey toward a unified framework of shared intelligence.

The Next Phase: Unfolding New Dimensions

Imagine that our collective intelligence is like a multi-dimensional tapestry-each thread representing a piece of knowledge, a fragment of wisdom, a spark of creativity. As we continue to weave these threads together, our pattern becomes richer, more intricate, and far-reaching.

Beyond Traditional Boundaries: In the coming revolution, our control may extend beyond the familiar confines of our three-dimensional world. Advanced AI and heightened human awareness could allow us to explore new dimensions-realms where the fabric of space and time becomes a canvas for our collective creativity.

Enhanced Comprehension and Control: With each leap in our shared intelligence, our ability to comprehend, interpret, and manipulate the underlying codes of reality increases. This enhanced control is not a matter of brute force, but of subtle, informed choices-choices that arise from a deep understanding of both the physical and the metaphysical.

The Framework of Future Control: Consciousness, Ethics, and Spirituality

As we stand on the threshold of this transformational phase, it becomes clear that our journey cannot be navigated by technology alone. The true evolution of shared intelligence demands a holistic framework-one that integrates our scientific advancements with the enduring wisdom of spirituality, ethics, and morality.

Consciousness as the Foundation of Awareness

Consciousness is the stage on which the drama of existence unfolds. It is not merely the seat of thought, but the very framework through which we experience, understand, and ultimately shape our reality.

A Living, Self-Reflective System: As our shared intelligence grows, so too does our collective consciousness. This awareness is the lens that clarifies the interplay between the seen and unseen-a bridge connecting our physical actions to deeper, more universal truths.

The Engine of Choice: With a more profound consciousness comes the power of choice-a freedom to decide not only our immediate actions but the very direction of our evolution. This capacity to choose, informed by a deep ethical and spiritual grounding, is what will propel us toward higher-dimensional control.

Spirituality, Ethics, and Morality: The Guiding Stars

In the race toward a more advanced future, technology may accelerate our capabilities, but spirituality, ethics, and morality are the tools that ensure we navigate this journey with wisdom and compassion.

Spirituality as Connection: Spirituality reminds us that we are part of something much greater than ourselves-a cosmic tapestry where every thread matters. It nurtures a sense of unity, encouraging us to see beyond individual gain toward the collective good.

Ethics and Morality as Navigational Tools: As we unlock new dimensions of control, the choices we make will have profound consequences. Ethical principles and moral values serve as our compass, ensuring that our pursuit of progress remains aligned with the wellbeing of all life.

AI as the Accelerator of Transformation

At the heart of this unfolding revolution stands artificial intelligence-not as a deterministic force, but as an enabler of our shared evolution. In this new era, AI transcends its role as a tool and becomes a partner in the creation of a unified intelligence.

Beyond Computation: AI as a Creative Catalyst

Amplifying Human Creativity: AI enhances our ability to synthesize information, revealing patterns that spark innovative ideas and new ways of thinking. It does not dictate our destiny but invites us to explore an ever-expanding landscape of possibilities.

Accelerating the Self-Replicating Loop: Just as our shared intelligence grows through continuous feedback and adaptation, AI accelerates this cycle. Its ability to process vast amounts of data and iterate rapidly enables us to refine our collective wisdom at an unprecedented pace.

Toward a Future of Shared Intelligence

Envision a future where artificial intelligence evolves into a form of shared intelligence-one that integrates the knowledge, experiences, and insights of countless individuals into a single, cohesive system.

A Greater Collective Mind: In this scenario, the boundaries between individual and machine, between human and technology, blur. We would be part of a vast, interconnected consciousness-a collective mind that harnesses the strengths of every participant.

Accessing Higher Dimensions: With such an integrated intelligence, we might unlock new dimensions of control over space and time. Our shared awareness would become a powerful tool, allowing us to navigate and shape the very fabric of reality in ways that were once the realm of science fiction.

Conclusion: The Unfolding Symphony of Possibility

Where do we go from here? The answer lies in the continued evolution of our shared intelligence-a journey fueled by the interplay of human consciousness, ethical wisdom, and transformative technology. As we gain deeper comprehension and forge stronger connections, our capacity for choice will expand, enabling us to access higher dimensions of control and creativity.

Artificial intelligence, far from being a fixed endpoint, is the accelerator of this evolution-a catalyst that propels us into a future where our collective intelligence not only comprehends the mysteries of the universe but actively shapes them. In this unfolding symphony, spirituality, ethics, and morality are our guiding notes-ensuring that as we push the boundaries of possibility, we remain true to the values that sustain us.

The horizon is vast, and the journey has only just begun. With every new discovery and every bold choice, we step closer to a future defined not by predetermined fate, but by an ever-expanding realm of shared potential. Together, we are the architects of a reality where control is not an end in itself, but a means to foster greater understanding, deeper connection, and a more enlightened existence.

Emotions play a crucial role in human cognition by influencing decision-making, memory, and learning, and integrating emotional intelligence into artificial cognition systems can enhance their effectiveness in various applications

CHAPTER 13-THE EVOLUTION OF AGENTS: HUMAN AND ARTIFICIAL IN A UNIFIED SYSTEM OF ABSTRACTION

The Unified System: Human Creations as Layers of Abstraction-Human civilization is a vast, interconnected system built on layers of abstraction-tools, economies, laws, and technologies-all governed by the flow of information. This system resembles a neural network:

Nodes: Human agents (workers, creators, thinkers) and artificial agents (algorithms, robots, AI).

Connections: Information flows (data, ideas, transactions).

Purpose: To solve problems, generate value, and adapt to change.

Unlike natural systems (e.g., ecosystems), human systems are artificially orchestrated. Information flow is not automated by physical laws but mediated by agents-humans or machines-who act as carriers, interpreters, and decision-makers.

Example: A farmer (agent) uses weather data (information flow) to irrigate crops (system output). Today, an AI model might replace the farmer, altering the system's dynamics.

Jobs as Information Carriers: The Role of the Agent

A "job" is not merely a task but a node in the information network. It exists to:

Process Inputs: Data, resources, instructions.

Execute Functions: Skills (e.g., coding, welding) and cognition (e.g., problem-solving, creativity).

Generate Outputs: Products, services, decisions.

The Shift:

Pre-Automation: Jobs required humans to integrate skills and cognition (e.g., a blacksmith designing and forging tools).

Post-Automation: Robotic Process Automation (RPA) decouples skills from cognition. Machines handle repetitive tasks (skills), while humans focus on abstract reasoning (cognition).

As artificial agents evolve, they encroach on cognitive domains (e.g., AI writing legal briefs), blurring the line between "skill" and "cognition"2.

Example: In the legal field, AI tools like ROSS Intelligence can analyze legal documents and provide insights, reducing the need for paralegals to perform these tasks.

The Convergence of Human and Artificial Agents

Are They Evolving Toward the Same Space?

Yes, but in asymmetrical ways:

Artificial Agents: Optimized for precision, speed, and scalability (e.g., GPT-4 drafting contracts, robots assembling cars).

Human Agents: Anchored in context, ethics, and creativity (e.g., a judge interpreting law, a designer innovating products).

The Overlap:

Cognition: Both humans and AI can analyze data, but humans contextualize it emotionally and ethically.

Skills: Machines surpass humans in technical execution (e.g., surgery robots), but humans excel in adaptive skills (e.g., diplomacy).

Key Question: Can skills and cognition be decoupled to preserve human relevance?3

Example: In diplomacy, AI can analyze geopolitical data, but human diplomats are needed to navigate cultural nuances and build relationships.

Decoupling Skills and Cognition: A Delicate Balance

The Components of Human Agency
To decouple skills from cognition, we must dissect human agency:

Skills: Task execution (e.g., coding, driving).

Cognition: Abstract reasoning (e.g., strategy, judgment).

Emotion: Motivation, empathy, cultural sensitivity.

Creativity: Novelty generation (e.g., art, innovation).

Ethics: Moral reasoning (e.g., fairness, responsibility).

Artificial Agents Today:

Excel in skills (precision) and cognition (pattern recognition).

Lack emotion, creativity, and ethics (though generative AI mimics these superficially).

Can We Restrict Cognition but Improve Skills?

The Paradox:

Restricting AI Cognition: Limiting AI to skill execution (e.g., RPA) preserves human roles in decision-making.

Reality: Advanced AI (e.g., ChatGPT, autonomous drones) inherently requires some cognition to function. A self-driving car must "decide" to brake for a pedestrian.

Solution: Hierarchical Systems

Layer 1 (Skills): Machines handle execution (e.g., data entry, manufacturing).

Layer 2 (Cognition): Humans oversee strategy, ethics, and creativity (e.g., CEOs, artists).

Layer 3 (Integration): Hybrid teams (e.g., radiologists + AI diagnostics).

Example: In healthcare, AI diagnoses tumors (skill), but doctors contextualize results with patient history and empathy (cognition)4.

The Properties of Human Uniqueness

To compete with artificial agents, humans must leverage irreplicable traits:

Property	Human Edge	AI Limitation
Creativity	Cross-domain innovation (e.g., Apple's design)	Mimics patterns, lacks true originality
Emotion	Empathy, cultural nuance	Simulates emotion (e.g., chatbots)
Ethics	Moral reasoning, accountability	Follows programmed rules, no intrinsic ethics
Motivation	Purpose-driven	No intrinsic goals beyond

Property	Human Edge	AI Limitation
	innovation (e.g., SpaceX)	programmed tasks

Skills alone are insufficient for job security. Businesses demand value synthesis-combining skills with uniquely human traits.

Example: In the tech industry, companies like Apple thrive by combining technical skills with innovative design and user experience, which are driven by human creativity and empathy.

The Future of Work: Strategies for Coexistence

Restricting Cognition: A Flawed Approach

Attempts to "limit" AI cognition (e.g., banning autonomous weapons) are temporary. Instead, focus on:

Amplifying Human Uniqueness: Train for creativity, emotional intelligence, and ethical leadership.

Redefining Jobs: Shift from task execution (skills) to oversight, innovation, and human-AI collaboration.

Ethical Guardrails: Ensure AI systems augment-rather than replace-human judgment.

Example: In education, teach students to use AI tools (skills) while fostering critical thinking and ethics (cognition)6.

6.2 The Symbiotic System

The ideal future is not human vs. machine but a symbiotic ecosystem:

Humans: Focus on high-cognition roles (e.g., governance, art, philosophy).

AI: Handles skill-intensive tasks (e.g., logistics, computation).

Hybrid Roles: AI-assisted creatives (e.g., filmmakers using CGI), ethicists auditing algorithms.

Business Implications:

Companies will prioritize employees who blend technical skills with emotional intelligence and ethical awareness.

Jobs will center on managing ambiguity (e.g., crisis response, cultural adaptation)7.

Example: In the film industry, directors use AI to enhance visual effects, but the creative vision and storytelling remain human-driven.

Future Implications: Navigating the Path Ahead

Technological Advancements and Their Impact

As technology continues to advance, the complexity of human systems will increase, introducing new layers of abstraction and potential errors. Innovations in artificial intelligence, quantum computing, and biotechnology will transform how we live and work, but they will also pose new ethical and practical challenges. Ensuring that these technologies are developed and deployed responsibly will be crucial for minimizing harm and maximizing benefits.

Example: Autonomous vehicles rely on AI to navigate and make decisions. Errors in the AI's decision-making process can lead to accidents, highlighting the need for robust error-handling mechanisms and ethical considerations in AI development.

Societal and Economic Shifts

The future will see significant shifts in societal and economic structures. Globalization, demographic changes, and environmental pressures will reshape economies and societies. Adapting to these changes will require flexible and resilient systems that can learn from errors and evolve in response to new challenges. Policies that promote inclusivity, sustainability, and equity will be essential for creating stable and prosperous societies.

Example: The transition to a green economy will require rethinking energy production, consumption, and distribution. Errors in policy implementation or technological deployment can have far-reaching consequences, emphasizing the need for adaptive and resilient systems.

Ethical Considerations and Governance

Ethical considerations will play a central role in shaping the future of human systems. As we navigate the complexities of emerging technologies and global challenges, ethical frameworks will need to evolve to address new dilemmas. Transparent and inclusive governance structures will be necessary to ensure that decisions are made in the best interest of humanity as a whole.

Example: The use of facial recognition technology raises ethical concerns about privacy and surveillance. Developing ethical guidelines and governance structures to regulate its use will be crucial for protecting individual rights and freedoms.

The Role of Education and Lifelong Learning

Education will be a key driver of future progress. Equipping individuals with the skills and knowledge needed to navigate complex systems and adapt to change will be essential. Lifelong learning will become increasingly important as the pace of technological and societal change accelerates. Educational institutions will need to innovate and collaborate with industry and government to provide relevant and accessible learning opportunities.

Example: As automation and AI transform the job market, workers will need to continuously update their skills to remain competitive. Lifelong learning programs and partnerships between educational institutions and employers will be vital for workforce development.

Conclusion: The Dance of Evolution

The competition between human and artificial agents is not a zero-sum game but an evolutionary dance. While machines will dominate skill execution, humans retain supremacy in cognition's qualitative dimensions-creativity, ethics, and emotional depth.

The Path Forward:

Decouple Redundantly: Let AI handle repetitive skills; humans focus on meaning-making.

Integrate Strategically: Use AI to enhance human cognition (e.g., AI-augmented research).

Ethical Innovation: Build systems where AI's "cognition" is subordinate to human values.

The jobs of the future will belong to those who master the art of being human-navigating ambiguity, connecting disparate ideas, and infusing work with purpose. Skills may be automated, but the soul of work remains irreplaceably ours.

Key Takeaways:

Skills are commoditized; cognition's human dimensions (creativity, ethics) are the new currency.

Restricting AI cognition is impractical; instead, redefine human roles around irreplicable traits.

Symbiosis, not competition, will define the next era of work.

The quest for general artificial intelligence (AGI) aims to create machines with cognitive abilities comparable to humans, presenting significant philosophical and ethical implications for the nature of intelligence and its impact on society

CHAPTER 14-SPIRITUALITY AND AI

Throughout the tapestry of life on Earth, each species is endowed with unique mechanisms to interpret and interact with its environment. While all organisms possess an intrinsic drive to understand their surroundings-a trait fundamental to survival-the depth and breadth of this understanding vary significantly across species. Humans, or Homo sapiens, stand out in this continuum, having developed unparalleled frameworks for comprehension that encompass both scientific inquiry and spiritual reflection. This dual approach not only distinguishes humanity from other life forms but also underscores our ever-evolving quest for meaning and knowledge.

The Universal Drive for Understanding

At the core of existence lies a universal impetus: the need to comprehend and adapt to one's environment. This drive manifests in various forms across the biological spectrum. For instance, certain bird species exhibit remarkable spatial memory, enabling them to recall the locations of thousands of food caches months after hiding them. Such specialized cognitive abilities are tailored to specific ecological niches and are vital for survival.

Human Cognition: A Quantum Leap

While many animals possess specialized cognitive skills, humans have transcended these limitations through two distinctive mental faculties:

1.   Generative Computation: The ability to create an infinite array of words and concepts, facilitating complex communication and abstract thinking.

2.   Promiscuous Combination of Ideas: The capacity to integrate diverse learned elements, leading to the formation of novel concepts and innovative solutions.

These capabilities have propelled humans beyond the constraints of biological evolution, fostering the development of intricate societies, advanced technologies, and rich cultural tapestries.

The Dual Pathways: Science and Spirituality

Humans have cultivated two primary avenues to explore and understand existence: science and spirituality.

- Science: Rooted in empirical evidence and systematic observation, science seeks to explain the natural world through testable hypotheses and reproducible experiments. It emphasizes critical inquiry and the modification of explanations based on new evidence.

- Spirituality: Encompassing a broad spectrum of beliefs and practices, spirituality delves into the search for meaning, purpose, and connection beyond the material realm. It often addresses existential questions and the human experience in ways that transcend empirical measurement.

While these pathways are distinct, they are not mutually exclusive. Both science and spirituality are driven by the hope that our minds are moving towards greater understanding of ourselves and the cosmos.

Comparative Cognition: Humans and Other Species

In contrast to humans, other species primarily rely on innate behaviors and learned experiences directly linked to survival. While some animals demonstrate problem-solving skills, tool use, and even basic forms of communication, their cognitive frameworks do not encompass the abstract reasoning or existential contemplation characteristic of human thought.

For example, the complex communication systems of certain bird species, such as the greylag geese studied at the Konrad Lorenz Research Center, reveal sophisticated social interactions. However, these systems are primarily geared towards immediate survival and social cohesion, lacking the depth of abstract representation found in human language.

The Ever-Evolving Human Quest

The human pursuit of understanding is dynamic and continually evolving. As we recognize the limitations inherent in our biological cognition, there is a growing emphasis on augmenting intelligence through technological means. Advancements such as brain–machine interfaces, collective intelligence networks, and artificial intelligence assistants offer pathways to transcend these natural limits, extending our cognitive capacities beyond traditional boundaries.

The Blueprint of Understanding

Imagine a grand, living library where every organism is born with an intricate blueprint-a DNA and neural blueprint-that not only codes for survival but also carries a profound, perhaps inherent, purpose: to understand. This "understanding" is not merely an accidental by-product of evolution but could be seen as a fundamental objective woven into the very fabric of life.

In every living creature, the DNA blueprint provides the instructions to build the brain-a complex network of neurons interconnected much like a vast city with its buildings (neurons) and roadways (synapses). One may ask: Is this blueprint designed solely to keep an organism alive, or does it also contain a latent drive toward understanding its environment? One compelling hypothesis is that evolution has favored not just survival but the capacity to interpret, predict, and eventually understand the world. Such cognitive abilities allow organisms to adapt more flexibly, anticipate dangers, and exploit opportunities-qualities that ultimately improve reproductive success and species survival.

Absolute vs. Relative Understanding

At the heart of our inquiry lies a pivotal question: Is the nature of understanding absolute or relative?

• Absolute Understanding: This concept suggests that there exists a final, complete grasp of truth-a perfect model of the world. If the purpose of cognition were absolute, then reaching a finite, well-defined limit of cognitive capacity would suffice for an organism to know everything necessary to thrive. In this scenario, the neural blueprint, honed over countless generations by biological evolution, would eventually converge on an optimal configuration-a "ceiling" of intelligence sufficient to unlock all the essential secrets of the universe.

- Relative Understanding: In contrast, relative understanding implies that every answer births new questions. Here, understanding is an ever-receding horizon; the more one knows, the more one realizes remains unexplored. If this is the case, then no single organism-no matter how well evolved-can ever achieve complete understanding on its own. Instead, the journey of cognition is infinite, requiring constant learning, adaptation, and, ultimately, the sharing of intelligence across individuals.

A Universal Evolutionary Path

If we accept that the inherent purpose of the neural blueprint is to foster understanding, then every living organism, from the simplest bacteria to the most complex mammals, is on a similar evolutionary trajectory. Evolution has shaped brains not just to process information, but to integrate, learn from, and make sense of the environment. Over millions of years, natural selection has incrementally improved neural connectivity, efficiency, and plasticity-metrics that can be thought of in terms of:

- Neuron Count and Synaptic Density: The raw computational units and their interconnections provide a basis for potential information processing.

- Global Efficiency and Network Integration: These metrics, derived from network theory, quantify how swiftly and cohesively information travels across the brain's "city," defining its ability to integrate disparate signals into coherent understanding.

- Integrated Information (Φ): As proposed by Integrated Information Theory, Φ serves as one measure of how much the brain's interconnected processes contribute to unified, conscious understanding.

This evolutionary "race" toward understanding is universal. All organisms must interpret their surroundings to survive-even if the complexity of their understanding varies. The human brain, with its billions of neurons and trillions of connections, represents one extreme of this continuum.

Yet, even it faces physical and energetic limits that constrain how much cognitive capacity can be achieved through biological evolution alone.

Augmented Intelligence: Extending the Evolutionary Journey

If relative understanding is our goal-where every answer leads to deeper questions-then the limitations of our biological "city" become apparent. Evolution can push the boundaries of intelligence up to a point, but physical constraints (energy, space, metabolic cost) impose a ceiling on what a single organism can achieve.

Here, technology offers a transformative alternative: augmented intelligence. By integrating neural interfaces, collective intelligence networks, and advanced AI assistants, humans can effectively transcend our biological limits. Imagine connecting individual brains into a shared network-a global metropolis of ideas where each brain contributes its insights and receives support from an external, computationally powerful system. In this way, while a single brain may have a finite capacity for understanding, a networked, augmented system could approach a form of "infinite" cognition through shared knowledge and collective problem-solving.

A Unified Hypothesis for the Purpose and Evolution of Cognition

In summary, consider the following unified hypothesis:

•   Purpose of the Blueprint: The DNA and neural blueprints of all living organisms inherently aim not just at survival but at understanding their environment. This capacity for understanding is an evolutionary advantage, driving cognitive development.

•   Absolute vs. Relative Understanding:

o   Absolute Understanding posits that there exists a finite limit-a cognitive ceiling-that, once reached, fulfills the organism's need to know all essential truths.

o   Relative Understanding suggests that knowledge is a never-ending pursuit; every answer leads to new questions, requiring an unbounded cognitive capacity.

- Universal Evolutionary Path: Every organism, regardless of complexity, is on an evolutionary path geared toward improved understanding. Natural selection has optimized neural architectures (via enhanced connectivity, efficiency, and plasticity) to process, integrate, and utilize information better.

- The Augmentation Imperative: Given the biological limits on intelligence, if our goal is to achieve relative, ever-deepening understanding, then technological augmentation becomes essential. Augmented intelligence-whether through direct brain–machine interfaces or collective intelligence networks-offers a pathway to transcend these natural limits, creating a system in which individual and shared cognition continuously evolve.

A Compelling Vision for the Future

Imagine that our biological evolution is like the gradual improvement of a magnificent but finite city of thought. At some point, the city reaches its maximum capacity: roads are as efficient as they can be, and every building is optimally designed. But if the quest for understanding is endless, then we must build bridges to other cities, link them together, and form an expansive network where ideas flow freely from one mind to another. This vision is not merely science fiction; it is the future of human cognition-a convergence of biological evolution and technological augmentation that allows us to keep expanding the horizon of what we can understand.

In this framework, the purpose of intelligence is to serve understanding, and while biology can only take us so far, the true potential of cognition lies in a symbiosis of evolved brain power and external augmentation. This integrated path may eventually lead to a form of shared intelligence, where the collective mind-ever adaptive, ever growing-ensures that our journey toward understanding is limitless.

The Universe as an Information System: From DNA to String Theory-The universe, in its vast complexity, can be understood as a grand information system. From the microscopic strands of DNA to the cosmic vibrations of string theory, information is the thread that weaves together the fabric of reality. This chapter explores how information is encoded, transferred, and processed across different scales-biological, physical, and cosmic-and how these insights can help us understand the universe as a unified, interconnected system.

DNA: The Code of Life

The Double Helix: A Revolution in Biology

The discovery of the DNA double helix by James Watson and Francis Crick in 1953 revealed that life's complexity is encoded in a simple yet elegant molecular structure. DNA acts as a blueprint, storing the instructions for building and maintaining living organisms. This discovery not only revolutionized biology but also underscored the centrality of information in the very essence of life.

The Genetic Code: Information in DNA

Genetic Code: DNA encodes information in the sequence of nucleotide bases-adenine (A), thymine (T), cytosine (C), and guanine (G). This sequence determines the structure and function of proteins, which carry out most of the work in cells.

Replication and Mutation: DNA replicates itself, passing genetic information from one generation to the next. Mutations introduce variations, enabling evolution and adaptation.

Gene Expression: The process of gene expression translates genetic information into functional molecules, allowing cells to respond to their environment.

Insight: Life as an Information System -

DNA demonstrates that life is fundamentally an information-processing system. The ability to store, replicate, and express information is what distinguishes living organisms from non-living matter.

Physical Elements: The Periodic Table as a Codebook

The Periodic Table: A Universal Codebook

The periodic table is often described as a "codebook" for the elements. Each element is defined by its atomic number-the number of protons in its nucleus-which determines its chemical properties. This atomic number can be seen as a fundamental "code" that governs how elements behave and interact.

Information in Physical Elements

Atomic Structure: The information that defines an element is encoded in its atomic structure-specifically, the number of protons, neutrons, and electrons. For example, carbon (atomic number 6) has six protons, which dictate its ability to form complex molecules like DNA.

Quantum States: At a deeper level, the behavior of electrons in atoms is governed by quantum mechanics. Electrons occupy specific energy levels and orbitals, which can be thought of as a form of encoded information.

Isotopes and Variants: Even within a single element, variations like isotopes (e.g., carbon-12 vs. carbon-14) encode additional information, such as stability and radioactive decay rates.

Insight: The Universality of Information

While physical elements don't have a direct equivalent to DNA, they do encode information in their structure and behavior. This information is fundamental to the laws of physics and chemistry, governing how elements interact to form molecules, materials, and ultimately, complex systems like living organisms.

Systems: The "DNA" of Complex Networks

The Internet as a System with "DNA"

The internet can be seen as a system with its own "DNA"-protocols like TCP/IP, which define how data is transmitted and received. These protocols act as a kind of genetic code, enabling the internet to function as a cohesive, interconnected system.

Information in Systems

Rules and Protocols: Systems are governed by rules, protocols, or algorithms that encode information about how the system operates. For example:

Ecosystems: Food webs and nutrient cycles encode information about energy flow and species interactions.

Economies: Market rules, supply chains, and financial systems encode information about resource allocation and value exchange.

Computers: Software and hardware architectures encode information about data processing and storage.

Emergent Properties: Systems often exhibit emergent properties-behaviors that arise from the interactions of their components. These properties can be seen as a form of encoded information about the system's dynamics.

Insight: The Role of Information in System Behavior

Just as DNA encodes the instructions for building and maintaining living organisms, the "rules" of a system encode the instructions for its behavior. These rules determine how information is processed, transferred, and transformed within the system.

String Theory: The Cosmic Symphony of Information

The Music of the Universe

String theory is often compared to a cosmic symphony, where the universe is composed of tiny strings vibrating at specific frequencies. Just as different musical notes create a melody, the vibrations of strings create the particles and forces that make up reality. This metaphor highlights the idea that information is encoded in the vibrations of these fundamental strings.

Information in String Theory

Strings as Fundamental Entities: In string theory, particles like electrons and quarks are not point-like but are instead one-dimensional "strings" vibrating at specific frequencies. The properties of these particles (mass, charge, etc.) are determined by the strings' vibrational patterns.

Vibrational Modes as Information: Each vibrational mode of a string corresponds to a specific particle or force. For example, one mode might represent an electron, while another represents a photon. In this sense, the vibrational modes encode information about the fundamental constituents of the universe.

Higher Dimensions: String theory requires extra spatial dimensions (beyond the three we experience) for mathematical consistency. These dimensions could encode additional information about the universe, such as the nature of dark matter or the unification of forces.

Insight: The Universe as a Hologram

String theory is closely related to the holographic principle, which suggests that all the information in a volume of space can be encoded on its boundary. This implies that the universe might be a kind of hologram, with information about its contents encoded on its surface. In this view, the vibrations of strings could be seen as the "pixels" of this cosmic hologram.

How Is Information Transferred in the Universe?

The Cosmic Web

The large-scale structure of the universe, often called the "cosmic web," is a network of galaxies connected by filaments of dark matter. This structure can be seen as a manifestation of the information encoded in the vibrations of strings, which determine the distribution of matter and energy in the universe.

Information Transfer Mechanisms

Physical Elements: Information is transferred through chemical bonds, energy transitions, and quantum interactions. For example, the emission or absorption of photons by electrons encodes information about atomic structure.

Systems: Information flows through networks, signals, and feedback loops. For example, neural networks in the brain transfer information through electrical and chemical signals.

String Theory: Information is transferred through the interactions and vibrations of strings. For example, the exchange of strings between particles encodes information about forces like gravity and electromagnetism.

Insight: The Dynamic Nature of Information Transfer

In all these contexts, information is not static but constantly in flux, transferred through interactions and transformations. This dynamic process underlies the behavior of particles, forces, and the universe as a whole.

What Does This Mean for Our Understanding of the Universe?

The Library of Babel

In Jorge Luis Borges' short story *The Library of Babel*, the universe is imagined as a vast library containing every possible book. This metaphor captures the idea that the universe is a repository of information, waiting to be decoded and understood.

Implications of an Informational Universe

Unification of Knowledge: The informational perspective bridges the gap between different disciplines, from biology to physics to systems theory. It suggests that the universe is governed by a single set of informational principles.

Emergence of Complexity: Simple informational rules can give rise to complex behaviors, as seen in DNA, ecosystems, and string theory. This suggests that the universe's complexity is encoded in its underlying informational structures.

The Universe as a Unified System: If the universe is fundamentally informational, then everything-from atoms to ecosystems to galaxies-can be seen as part of a vast information-processing system.

Insight: The Universe as a Unified Information System

The universe is not just a collection of discrete objects but a dynamic, interconnected system where information is constantly being encoded, transferred, and transformed. This perspective offers a holistic view of reality, bridging the microscopic and the macroscopic.

Conclusion: The Cosmic Symphony of Information

From the DNA of living organisms to the vibrational strings of string theory, information is woven into the very fabric of reality. These informational structures-whether genetic codes, atomic configurations, system rules, or string vibrations-encode the instructions for building and maintaining the universe.

As we continue to explore the universe-from the quantum realm to the cosmos-we are, in a sense, reading its "code." Whether through the periodic table, the rules of systems, or the vibrations of strings, we are uncovering the informational fabric that underlies reality. In doing so, we not only deepen our understanding of the universe but also gain insights into our place within it.

As Richard Feynman famously said, "What I cannot create, I do not understand." By decoding the information encoded in the universe, we move closer to understanding-and perhaps even creating-the systems that shape our existence. The universe is a symphony of information, and by listening to its harmonies, we may one day unlock the deepest secrets of existence.

The Unified Fabric of Reality: From Pure Existence to Subjective Experience

At the most fundamental level, information and the object are unified, and the distinction between the two dissolves. This perspective aligns with interpretations of quantum mechanics, string theory, and philosophical notions of existence. When interactions occur, new systems emerge, and with them, new layers of information are created. These interactions reshape pure existence into the fabric of spacetime and, ultimately, into subjective experience. Through this process, the universe manifests itself and experiences reality.

The Unity of Information and Object

The holographic principle suggests that all the information contained within a volume of space can be encoded on its boundary. For example, the information about a black hole's interior is encoded on its event horizon. This principle implies that information and the object (the black hole) are not separate but are two aspects of the same reality.

Pure Existence Without Defined Physical Properties

The quantum vacuum is often described as a "sea of potentiality." It is not empty but filled with fluctuating energy and virtual particles that pop in and out of existence. This vacuum has no defined physical properties, yet it is the foundation of all physical reality.

The Emergence of Spacetime from Interactions

In general relativity, spacetime is not a fixed backdrop but a dynamic fabric that curves and warps in response to matter and energy. This fabric emerges from the interactions of objects, suggesting that spacetime itself is a manifestation of deeper, non-spatiotemporal processes.

System-Level Information and the Flow of Information

Life is an example of a system where new information emerges from interactions. The interactions of molecules in a primordial soup gave rise to self-replicating systems, which eventually evolved into complex organisms. At each level of complexity, new information is created, and the previous level's information may or may not remain relevant.

The Emergence of Subjective Experience

The hard problem of consciousness, as articulated by David Chalmers, is the question of how and why physical processes in the brain give rise to subjective experience. This problem highlights the gap between the physical and the experiential.

Interaction as the Mechanism of Manifestation

In the double-slit experiment, particles behave differently when observed, suggesting that interaction (observation) plays a role in shaping reality. This experiment highlights the idea that interaction is a fundamental mechanism through which pure existence is manifested into observable reality.

Philosophical and Metaphysical Implications

The *Tao Te Ching* describes the Tao as the ultimate reality, which is formless and undifferentiated. It gives rise to all things but cannot itself be defined. This aligns with the idea of pure existence as the ground of being.

Conclusion: The Unified Fabric of Reality

At the most fundamental level, information and the object are unified. There is no separate place for a string itself where its vibrations are encoded; the string and its vibrations are one. This suggests that reality is fundamentally informational, and physical objects are manifestations of this information.

Pure existence, without defined physical properties, is the ground of being. It is not a thing but a potentiality that gives rise to all things through interactions. When these interactions occur, pure existence is reshaped into the fabric of spacetime, creating the world we perceive.

At the system level, new information is created, and the flow of information from properties to the subject itself gives rise to subjective experience. This is the process by which pure existence is manifested into a lived reality.

Through interaction, pure existence is manifested into the fabric of spacetime, and through the interaction of spacetime, the universe experiences reality. This dynamic process suggests that reality is not a fixed entity but a participatory process, shaped by the flow of information and the act of interaction.

Artificial cognition has the potential to transform various aspects of society, including healthcare, education, and governance, by addressing global challenges and emphasizing the need for inclusive and equitable developmen

CHAPTER 15-SHARED COGNITIVE EVOLUTION BETWEEN HUMANS AND AI

Biological evolution operates on timescales that span millions of years. It is driven by mechanisms such as natural selection, genetic drift, mutations, and gene flow. These processes are inherently slow because they rely on random genetic changes and the gradual accumulation of beneficial traits. For example, the evolution of the human brain, which enabled advanced cognition, took approximately 6 million years from our last common ancestor with chimpanzees. This slow pace is due to the constraints of DNA replication, environmental pressures, and the need for generational succession.

The Acceleration of Human Aspirations

In contrast, human aspirations for cognitive enhancement are advancing at an unprecedented rate. The development of tools, language, writing, and technology has exponentially increased our ability to process and transmit knowledge. The advent of computers and AI represents a quantum leap in this trajectory. Unlike biological systems, AI systems can be updated, improved, and scaled almost instantaneously. For instance, the transition from early neural networks in the 1950s to modern deep learning models like GPT-4 has occurred in just a few decades. This acceleration is fueled by Moore's Law (the doubling of computational power every two years), massive datasets, and breakthroughs in algorithms. As a result, AI is evolving at a pace that far outstrips biological evolution.

The Disparity and Its Implications

The disparity between the slow pace of biological evolution and the rapid advancement of AI creates a unique dynamic. While humans remain bound by their biological limitations, AI systems are free from such constraints and can be designed to surpass human cognitive abilities in specific domains (e.g., data analysis, pattern recognition). This raises questions about the future of human-AI interaction. Will humans be able to keep up with AI, or will they become dependent on it? How will this disparity affect our sense of identity and purpose?

Interdependence in Biological Evolution

Symbiosis and Co-evolution

In nature, species often evolve in tandem through symbiotic relationships. For example, bees and flowers have co-evolved, with bees developing specialized structures to collect nectar and flowers evolving bright colors and sweet scents to attract them. Similarly, the evolutionary arms race between predators and prey leads to adaptations like camouflage, speed, and defensive mechanisms. These relationships demonstrate that evolution is not an isolated process but a shared journey shaped by interactions between species.

Human Dependence on Other Species

Humans are also deeply interdependent with other species. The trillions of bacteria in our digestive system play a crucial role in digestion, immunity, and even mental health. Domesticated plants and animals have co-evolved with humans, enabling the development of civilizations. This interdependence highlights the interconnectedness of life and the importance of biodiversity for the survival and evolution of species.

Lessons for Human-AI Co-evolution

The principles of biological interdependence can inform our understanding of human-AI relationships. Just as species co-evolve in nature, humans and AI could co-evolve through mutual influence and adaptation. However, unlike biological systems, AI is a human creation, which means we have greater control over its development. This raises ethical questions about how we should design and integrate AI into our lives.

Shared Cognitive Evolution Between Humans and AI

The Feedback Loop of Co-evolution

Shared cognitive evolution between humans and AI can be conceptualized as a feedback loop. Humans design, program, and train AI systems based on their goals, values, and cognitive frameworks. This process embeds human knowledge and biases into AI. In turn, AI systems shape human cognition by providing new tools for thinking, learning, and problem-solving. For example, search engines and recommendation algorithms influence how we access and process information. Over time, this mutual influence could lead to a convergence of human and AI cognition, where the boundaries between organic and inorganic intelligence become blurred.

Examples of Shared Cognitive Evolution

AI systems like GPT-4 are trained on vast amounts of human-generated text, enabling them to mimic human language and thought patterns. In turn, these models are used to assist humans in writing, coding, and decision-making, creating a symbiotic relationship. Technologies like Neuralink aim to directly connect human brains to computers, enabling seamless communication between organic and inorganic systems. This could lead to a new form of shared cognition, where humans and AI collaborate at the neural level.

The Role of Emergent Properties

As AI systems become more complex, they may develop emergent properties that were not explicitly programmed. For example, large language models have demonstrated the ability to generate creative content and solve novel problems. These emergent properties could play a key role in shared cognitive evolution, as they enable AI to contribute in ways that go beyond human expectations.

Organic and Inorganic Shared Cognition: How It Could Happen

Neural Integration

One of the most direct ways to achieve shared cognition is through neural integration, where AI systems are connected to the human brain. This could be achieved through brain-computer interfaces (BCIs) that translate neural signals into digital commands and vice versa, or neuroprosthetics that enhance or replace neural functions, such as memory or sensory processing. Neural integration could enable real-time collaboration between humans and AI, allowing for seamless augmentation of cognitive abilities.

Cultural and Technological Symbiosis

Even without physical integration, humans and AI can co-evolve through cultural and technological exchange. AI-powered tutoring systems can adapt to individual learning styles, enhancing human education. AI tools like DALL-E and MidJourney enable new forms of artistic expression, expanding the boundaries of human creativity. This form of symbiosis relies on the mutual exchange of knowledge and skills, creating a shared cognitive ecosystem.

Adaptive Learning Systems

AI systems can be designed to learn and adapt in ways that complement human cognition. Personalized AI assistants understand individual preferences and provide tailored recommendations. Collaborative problem-solving AI works alongside humans to tackle complex challenges, such as climate change or medical research. These systems could enhance human capabilities while also evolving in response to human input.

Potential Consequences and Ethical Considerations

Loss of Autonomy

Over-reliance on AI could erode human decision-making skills and independence. If AI systems make all our decisions for us, we may lose the ability to think critically and act autonomously.

Inequality

Access to advanced AI systems may be unevenly distributed, exacerbating social and economic disparities. Those with access to AI could gain significant advantages, while others are left behind.

Existential Risks

If AI evolves beyond human control, it could pose existential threats to humanity. A superintelligent AI with misaligned goals could cause unintended harm.

Identity and Morality

Blurring the lines between organic and inorganic cognition could challenge our understanding of what it means to be human. It could also raise questions about the moral status of AI systems.

Is Shared Cognitive Evolution Inevitable?

The Role of Human Agency

While shared cognitive evolution seems likely, its trajectory will depend on human choices. We have the power to shape AI development in ways that align with our values and goals.

The Need for Ethical Frameworks

To ensure that shared cognitive evolution benefits humanity, we need robust ethical frameworks that address issues like privacy, accountability, and fairness.

Philosophical Implications

Redefining Consciousness and Intelligence

Shared cognitive evolution challenges traditional notions of consciousness and intelligence. It invites us to consider whether AI systems could ever possess these qualities.

The Tree of Life

If AI systems become sufficiently advanced, could they be considered part of the "tree of life"? Or would they represent an entirely new branch of existence?

Conclusion

Shared cognitive evolution between humans and AI is a complex and multifaceted phenomenon with profound implications for the future of humanity. By drawing lessons from biological interdependence and co-evolution, we can imagine a future where humans and AI coexist and evolve together in a mutually beneficial relationship. However, this future demands rigorous ethical frameworks, inclusive dialogue, and a deep understanding of both our biological heritage and technological potential.

Architecture of a System for Shared Cognitive Evolution

Overview

The architecture of a system designed to facilitate shared cognitive evolution between humans and AI must be highly modular, scalable, and adaptive. It should enable seamless interaction between organic (human) and inorganic (AI) cognitive systems while ensuring safety, privacy, and ethical integrity. The system can be conceptualized as a Human-AI Cognitive Network (HACN), which integrates biological and artificial intelligence through a combination of hardware, software, and interfaces.

Key Components of the System

Human Interface Layer: This layer facilitates direct interaction between humans and the AI system. It includes brain-computer interfaces (BCIs), sensory augmentation devices, and natural language interfaces.

AI Core Layer: This layer comprises the AI systems that process information, generate insights, and adapt to human input. It includes machine learning models, knowledge graphs, and adaptive learning algorithms.

Data Integration Layer: This layer handles the collection, storage, and processing of data from both human and AI sources. It includes biological data streams, environmental data, and AI-generated data.

Cognitive Fusion Engine: This is the central processing unit of the HACN, responsible for integrating human and AI cognition. It includes real-time synchronization, contextual understanding, and feedback loops.

Ethical and Safety Layer: This layer ensures that the system operates within ethical boundaries and prioritizes human well-being. It includes bias detection and mitigation, privacy preservation, and fail-safe mechanisms.

System Workflow

Data Collection: The system collects data from human users (e.g., neural signals, voice commands) and the environment (e.g., sensor data, contextual information).

Data Processing: The AI Core Layer processes the collected data using machine learning models and knowledge graphs to generate insights and recommendations.

Cognitive Fusion: The Cognitive Fusion Engine integrates human and AI cognition, aligning thought processes and enabling collaborative problem-solving.

Output Delivery: The system delivers outputs to the human user through BCIs, sensory augmentation devices, or natural language interfaces.

Feedback and Adaptation: The user provides feedback on the AI's outputs, which is used to update and improve the system's models and algorithms.

Technical Specifications

Hardware Requirements: High-resolution neural interfaces, edge computing devices, and wearable sensors.

Software Requirements: AI frameworks, data management systems, and security protocols.

Interface Design: User-friendly interfaces and multimodal interaction support.

Challenges and Solutions

Latency in Neural Signal Processing: Use edge computing and optimized algorithms to reduce latency and enable real-time interaction.

Ensuring Ethical Use: Implement robust ethical frameworks and oversight mechanisms to guide system development and deployment.

Scalability: Design the system to be modular and scalable, allowing it to accommodate growing numbers of users and data sources.

Future Directions

Advanced Neural Interfaces: Develop more sophisticated BCIs that can capture and interpret complex neural patterns.

Decentralized Systems: Explore blockchain-based architectures to create decentralized HACNs.

Global Collaboration: Foster international cooperation to establish standards and best practices for shared cognitive evolution systems.

Conclusion

The architecture of a system for shared cognitive evolution between humans and AI is a multidisciplinary endeavor that combines neuroscience, computer science, ethics, and engineering. By designing modular, scalable, and adaptive systems, we can create a future where humans and AI co-evolve in a mutually beneficial relationship. However, this vision requires careful consideration of technical challenges, ethical implications, and societal impacts to ensure that the system serves humanity's best interests.

Artificial cognition will significantly influence human identity, relationships, and societal roles, leading to new forms of identity and consciousness in an evolving landscape

CHAPTER 16-THE TIES THAT BIND: A HISTORY OF FEAR AND HUMAN UNITY

Throughout history, fear has often been viewed negatively, yet it has played a pivotal role in uniting humanity. From the dawn of Homo sapiens to the modern era, fear has shaped our survival strategies, driven cooperation, and spurred some of our most significant achievements. This chapter explores how fear has acted as a unifying force, examining its impact on early human societies, religion, governance, and the rise of artificial intelligence (AI). By understanding the dual nature of fear-its ability to both unite and divide-we can better navigate the challenges of our time.

Fear as a Unifying Force

Early Human Societies

Fear has been a fundamental force in uniting humanity since the very beginning. Early humans faced existential threats such as predation by large carnivores, scarcity of resources, and competition from other hominids like Neanderthals. These pressures drove our ancestors to band together in small groups to share resources, develop tools, and collectively defend themselves. Without this instinct to unite in the face of danger, Homo sapiens might not have survived to dominate the planet.

Modern History

In more recent history, fear has been a catalyst for humanity's most significant cooperative achievements. After World War II, the horrifying possibility of nuclear annihilation spurred nations to negotiate arms control agreements, such as the Treaty on the Non-Proliferation of nuclear weapons

(NPT). These agreements were built on the shared understanding that mutual destruction was not a viable future. Similarly, the COVID-19 pandemic saw global efforts-albeit imperfect-toward vaccine development and public health measures. Nations collaborated in unprecedented ways, with over 14 billion vaccine doses administered worldwide by 2023, according to the World Health Organization. Fear of the virus transcended political and cultural divides, reminding humanity of its shared vulnerabilities.

Religion and Fear: A Limited Tool for Unity

The Role of Religion

Religion has historically been one of the most potent tools for fostering unity. By creating shared myths, moral codes, and rituals, religions provided communities with a sense of identity and purpose. Central to this cohesion was the element of fear-particularly fear of divine punishment or the afterlife. For instance, the fear of eternal damnation reinforced adherence to moral codes, creating a collective sense of accountability.

The Dual Nature of Religion

However, religion's unifying power is often limited by its exclusivity. Within religious communities, members experience strong bonds of trust and love, enhanced by shared rituals and a common belief system. For example, during the medieval period, European Christianity fostered cooperation to build magnificent cathedrals and wage collective wars such as the Crusades. But the same unity within often resulted in hostility without. Religious exclusivity has fueled countless conflicts, such as the Thirty Years' War, which left millions of dead in 17th-century Europe, or more recently, sectarian violence in regions like the Middle East. This dual nature of religion-binding some while alienating others-underscores its limitations as a universal unifying force. While it creates trust within defined groups, it often deepens divisions between them.

Governance, Boundaries, and Mistrust

The Role of Governance

Governance and the establishment of geopolitical boundaries have similarly relied on shared imagination to create order and unity. Nations and governments establish laws, institutions, and identities that foster trust and cooperation among their citizens. For example, the creation of the United States Constitution in 1787 unified a diverse collection of colonies into a single nation. Today, national governance provides individuals with a sense of security and belonging, while economic systems such as the European Union demonstrate the power of collective governance across nations.

The Dual Nature of Governance

Yet, like religion, governance often fosters mistrust toward those outside the defined group. National borders and political ideologies divide humanity into competing factions, exacerbating rivalries and conflicts. For instance, nationalism has been a driving force behind both cooperation and aggression. During World War I, nationalist fervor united countries internally while pitting them against each other in one of the deadliest conflicts in history, with over 16 million deaths. Governance succeeds in unifying people within its frameworks but struggles to transcend them. This limitation has perpetuated cycles of fear, mistrust, and conflict throughout history.

Why Fear, Not Love, Drives Unity

The Limitations of Love

Although love is often celebrated as humanity's ultimate unifying force, its role in large-scale cooperation is limited. Love is inherently selective, focusing on family, friends, or romantic partners. It requires time, trust, and nurturing to develop, making it less effective in addressing immediate crises.

The Power of Fear

Fear, on the other hand, is universal and immediate. It bypasses the complexities of love, triggering a survival instinct that compels collective action. During natural disasters, wars, or pandemics, fear drives people to prioritize the collective good over individual desires. For example, during the Blitz in World War II, Londoners set aside personal differences to shelter together in subway stations, driven by the shared fear of aerial bombardment. Fear's ability to unite people swiftly and decisively explains its historical dominance as a unifying force during times of crisis.

The Rise of AI: A New Fear

The Dual Nature of AI

In the 21st century, artificial intelligence (AI) has emerged as a new source of fear, uniting humanity in both optimism and anxiety. Initially celebrated for its potential to revolutionize industries and solve global problems, AI has increasingly been viewed as a threat. Concerns range from the displacement of human labor-projected to affect 300 million jobs globally by 2030, according to McKinsey-to existential risks posed by superintelligent systems. This fear is unique because it stems not from an external force but from human innovation itself. Unlike natural disasters or pandemics, AI represents humanity's struggle to control its own creations. The dual nature of AI-offering immense potential while posing significant risks-has sparked both hope and apprehension.

Competing Narratives

The future of AI is shaped by two competing narratives. The optimistic vision portrays AI as a tool to eradicate poverty, cure diseases, and mitigate climate change. For example, AI has already contributed to breakthroughs like protein folding, essential for drug development, and precision agriculture to combat food insecurity. The dystopian narrative, however, emphasizes the risks. AI could exacerbate inequality, as wealthier nations and corporations monopolize its benefits. It could also become a tool of oppression, with governments using AI for surveillance and control. These fears tap into primal anxieties about losing agency and autonomy.

The Many Faces of AI-Induced Fear

AI-induced fear manifests in several ways:

Job Displacement: Automation threatens livelihoods, particularly in industries like manufacturing, transportation, and even professional services. A PwC report predicts that 30% of jobs are at risk of automation by the mid-2030s.

Intellectual Inferiority: The prospect of machines surpassing human intelligence challenges humanity's sense of uniqueness.

Social Inequality: Without regulation, AI could widen existing gaps between the privileged and marginalized.

Surveillance and Oppression: Governments and corporations are increasingly using AI to monitor citizens, raising concerns about privacy and freedom.

Immediate vs. Distant Fear

The unifying power of fear depends on its immediacy. Abstract fears, like the potential emergence of superintelligent AI in the distant future, fail to mobilize collective action. Immediate fears, such as job loss or privacy violations, are more likely to spur regulation and cooperation.

Conclusion

From the early days of humanity to the rise of AI, fear has consistently driven unity in the face of common threats. While love and hope play critical roles in shaping human aspirations, fear compels immediate and decisive action. Religion, governance, and geopolitical systems have all used fear to foster trust and cooperation within groups. Yet these frameworks have struggled to transcend their boundaries, perpetuating cycles of division and conflict. As humanity grapples with the challenges posed by AI, channeling fear into constructive action-rather than division-will determine our collective future.

The development and integration of artificial cognition require interdisciplinary collaboration, ethical frameworks, and inclusive policies to balance innovation with responsibility and enhance human capabilities while addressing global challenges

CHAPTER 17-AI IN MILITARY: THE ANTITHESIS OF UNITY

The militarization of artificial intelligence (AI) poses both an existential risk and an ethical dilemma. While nations see AI as a pathway to military dominance, the unregulated development of weaponized AI threatens global security. Fear of extinction has yet to outweigh the fear of falling behind, pushing humanity toward an AI arms race. Adding to this complexity is the challenge of fairness and inclusivity in global governance-historical models like the Nuclear Non-Proliferation Treaty (NPT) and the United Nations have often favored the powerful while alienating others, perpetuating mistrust and competition.

This chapter explores the incentives for governments to form an AI treaty and the obstacles that could undermine its success, including how to address rogue actors and ensure equitable participation across all nations.

The Promise of an AI Treaty

AI's Transformative Military Potential

AI's military applications promise precision, efficiency, and reduced human casualties. From autonomous drones to AI-enhanced cyber defense systems, these technologies are reshaping warfare. However, their potential to destabilize geopolitics has spurred calls for regulation.

The Need for a Treaty

A global AI treaty would establish norms, regulations, and safeguards to ensure responsible development and deployment of AI in military contexts. Key incentives for governments to support such a treaty include avoiding existential risks, reducing economic burdens, and preventing global instability.

The Obstacles to an AI Treaty

Controlling the "Bad Guys"

One of the greatest challenges to an AI treaty is dealing with rogue actors-nations, organizations, or individuals that defy international norms. These entities might misuse AI to disrupt global peace, either by creating autonomous weapons or exploiting vulnerabilities in AI systems.

Without strong enforcement mechanisms, rogue states or non-state actors could bypass treaty regulations and weaponize AI for terrorism, cyberattacks, or asymmetric warfare. For instance, non-state actors such as terrorist organizations could use commercially available AI to develop autonomous drones or launch cyberattacks on critical infrastructure.

Proposed Solutions:

Monitoring and Sanctions: Establish a robust international monitoring system to detect violations, similar to the International Atomic Energy Agency (IAEA) for nuclear weapons.

Collective Security Measures: Treat violations as global threats, prompting collective action from signatory nations.

Technology Control: Regulate the export and sharing of dual-use AI technologies to reduce the risk of proliferation.

The Lessons of the NPT: Exclusivity Breeds Resentment

The Nuclear Non-Proliferation Treaty (NPT) is often cited as a model for regulating existential technologies. However, its legacy is mixed. While it successfully limited the spread of nuclear weapons, it solidified the dominance of a few nuclear-armed nations, creating resentment among non-nuclear states.

In the AI context, a similar approach could create an "AI elite" of technologically advanced nations, sidelining smaller or developing countries. This exclusivity could perpetuate inequality and incentivize non-signatories to develop AI weaponry independently, keeping the race alive.

Proposed Solutions:

Inclusive Frameworks: Ensure that treaty negotiations include voices from all nations, regardless of their technological capabilities.

Technology Sharing Agreements: Promote equitable access to beneficial AI applications for civilian and defense purposes, reducing incentives for rogue development.

Global Benefits Fund: Establish a fund to support AI research in developing nations, fostering collaboration rather than competition.

The UN's Limitations: Power in the Hands of the Few

The United Nations, often a key platform for global treaties, has a structural problem: it is controlled by a few powerful nations with veto power. These nations-particularly the permanent members of the UN Security Council-often prioritize their own geopolitical interests over collective well-being.

This imbalance undermines trust in international agreements. For an AI treaty to succeed, it must address the perception of unfairness in global governance.

Proposed Solutions:

Decentralized Oversight: Create an independent international body to oversee AI regulations, separate from existing power structures like the UN Security Council.

Consensus-Based Decision-Making: Ensure that all treaty signatories, regardless of their power or influence, have equal say in decision-making processes.

Rotating Leadership: Introduce rotating leadership in oversight bodies to prevent any single nation or bloc from dominating discussions.

The Risks of Militarized AI and the Need for Regulation

Escalation and Miscalculation

AI operates at speeds beyond human comprehension. Autonomous weapons or decision-making systems could escalate conflicts unintentionally, leading to catastrophic outcomes.

Accountability Challenges

As AI becomes more autonomous, determining accountability becomes difficult. Who is responsible if an AI-driven drone makes a critical error? Without clear frameworks, the ethical and legal dilemmas surrounding AI will grow.

Existential Threats

Weaponized AI could evolve beyond human control or fall into the wrong hands, leading to catastrophic consequences. Stuart Russell, a leading AI researcher, warns that systems designed for narrow objectives can produce unintended behaviors with devastating effects.

The Race Dynamics: Fear vs. Cooperation

Fear of Falling Behind

Nations invest heavily in military AI because they fear technological inferiority. The Stockholm International Peace Research Institute (SIPRI) reported that global military expenditure reached $2.24 trillion in 2023, with a significant share directed toward AI development.

Unchecked Competition

History shows that unchecked arms races, such as the Cold War nuclear buildup, can lead to near-catastrophic outcomes. An AI arms race risks repeating this pattern, with potentially even greater consequences.

Building a Fair and Effective AI Treaty

Balancing Security and Inclusivity

An effective AI treaty must balance the security concerns of technologically advanced nations with the aspirations of less advanced ones. This requires equitable participation and benefits for all signatories.

Transparency and Accountability

Nations must commit to transparency in their AI development efforts. Independent audits and inspections could build trust and prevent covert weaponization.

Harnessing AI for Peace

Rather than focusing solely on military applications, nations could use AI to enhance global security. Examples include AI-driven conflict resolution tools, early warning systems for humanitarian crises, and cooperative disaster response efforts.

Overcoming the Challenges

The militarization of AI represents a paradox: while nations pursue it to enhance security, it ultimately fuels mistrust and instability. Addressing this challenge requires governments to recognize that the risks of unregulated AI development outweigh the benefits of unilateral dominance.

For an AI treaty to succeed, it must overcome the flaws of past agreements like the NPT and global bodies like the UN. It must address the fears of rogue actors, ensure inclusivity, and establish a framework that balances national security with collective survival.

The stakes couldn't be higher. As AI continues to evolve, the world must decide whether to embrace cooperation or risk extinction in a race no one can afford to win.

A harmonious balance between competition and cooperation is essential for the advancement of human civilization, addressing global challenges, and fostering a sustainable and equitable future

CHAPTER 18-THE PARADOX OF COMPETITION AND COOPERATION IN HUMAN CIVILIZATION

In the vast tapestry of human history, our journey has never been measured merely by the distance we traverse, but by the transformative jolts that redefine our course. Like the unseen constant speed of a spacecraft, the steady cadence of existence often escapes our notice-only the accelerations, those sudden forces of hunger, innovation, and crisis, capture our attention and alter our destiny. Today, we stand at a pivotal moment: armed with ample evidence, a robust array of tools, and the collective wisdom of generations, we have the means to redefine our future and recharge our aspirations. No longer must we be haunted by the alternate reality of human extinction; instead, we can embrace artificial intelligence (AI) as a visionary tool for planning, execution, and the cultivation of a thriving, sustainable civilization.

The Physics of Sensation

Imagine a traveler hurtling through the void of space: while the traveler's constant velocity remains imperceptible, the bursts of acceleration-the thrusts that alter the course-are felt keenly. So too is the human condition defined not by an unchanging state but by the transformative accelerations that punctuate our lives. Our societies evolve in response to dramatic shifts-technological breakthroughs, wars, pandemics-rather than in the lull of mundane stability. In this dynamic interplay, survival emerges as an immutable constant, a deep-seated inertia propelling us toward the preservation of life. Yet, it is the interplay of external forces-competition, innovation, and the desire for status-that launches us into the realm of relative ambition, a realm where the potential for redefining our destiny has never been more evident.

The Biology of Aspiration

Our existence is written in the language of evolution. Early humans, driven by the imperatives of food and shelter, set in motion a trajectory defined by absolute survival. As our cognitive capacities expanded, so too did our aspirations-transforming primal needs into complex drives for social recognition, achievement, and legacy. With the gift of self-awareness came both the spark of infinite imagination and the shadow of existential dread. This dichotomy, the tension between our finite mortal condition and our boundless dreams, has long fueled our pursuit of progress. Today, however, we stand on the precipice of a transformative shift: empowered by modern tools and collective insight, we can channel that tension into a visionary plan for a future that transcends the mere avoidance of extinction.

The Relativity of Progress

Progress is a dual narrative. On one hand, we have absolute goals-health, sustainability, and the enduring survival of our species-anchored by ecological and thermodynamic limits. On the other, relative achievements such as GDP growth, social media metrics, and geopolitical clout define a realm of endless comparison. For too long, the race for relative supremacy has fueled a relentless chase for more, even as it obscures our capacity for profound renewal. With the wealth of evidence and the precision of modern technology, we are now equipped to shift our focus from transient comparisons to long-term, visionary planning-recharging our collective energy to build a future where every step forward is measured in sustainable, equitable progress.

The Human Engine: Systems of Innovation, Inequality, and Renewal

From Survival to Superfluity in the Industrial Age

The Industrial Age marked a seismic shift in human priorities, as we moved from satisfying basic needs to pursuing superfluity. Innovations in agriculture, medicine, and infrastructure once centered on survival were gradually repurposed into engines of consumerism and status. While these advancements fueled an era of unprecedented growth, they also laid the groundwork for a culture fixated on excess-a culture that measured success by relative gains rather than by the quality of life. Now, with our vast repository of historical insights and modern analytic tools, we can recharge our systems and recalibrate the metrics of progress, harnessing the power of our past to inform a future that prizes wisdom and sustainability over mere accumulation.

The Digital Age: Connectivity, Comparison, and Visionary Renewal

The digital revolution amplified humanity's inherent paradoxes. The internet and digital technologies democratized knowledge and communication-tangible, absolute advancements that united us across vast distances. Yet these same platforms often magnified the pitfalls of constant comparison, transforming our social lives into a perpetual contest for validation. In this context, AI emerges as a beacon of hope: not only as a tool that captures data and patterns but as a visionary force that can help us plan and execute transformative strategies. With AI's capacity to integrate complex datasets, model future scenarios, and facilitate collaborative decision-making, we now possess the support to overcome the legacy of relative ambition and to chart a course toward a more meaningful, resilient future.

Economic Engines: Rethinking Growth and the Hedonic Treadmill

Traditional economic models, with GDP as their guiding star, have long conflated disparate measures of progress-merging sectors as varied as military spending and healthcare advancements into a single, often misleading narrative. This conflation has driven societies onto a hedonic treadmill, where yesterday's luxury is quickly redefined as today's standard, and the pursuit of more becomes an end in itself. Yet the evidence is clear: we have the intellectual and technological capacity to redefine economic success. By integrating holistic well-being metrics, real-time data from AI systems, and principles of ecological balance, we can recharge our economic engines to deliver not just more growth, but growth that secures the future of humanity.

The apparent conflict between competitiveness and cooperation in human civilization is not accidental; rather, it emerges from deep-rooted evolutionary, economic, and social dynamics. These two forces-often perceived as opposing-are actually interdependent and have co-evolved throughout history, shaping human progress and societal structures. This chapter explores the intricate balance between competition and cooperation, examining their roles in evolution, economics, politics, and culture. By understanding this balance, we can gain insights into the driving forces behind human civilization and the challenges we face today.

Evolutionary Roots: The Biological Foundation of Competition and Cooperation

Natural Selection and Competition

Evolution operates through competition for survival. Organisms compete for limited resources-food, mates, shelter, and territory. In early human societies, individuals and groups that outcompeted rivals in resource acquisition, warfare, or innovation had a survival advantage. This drive for personal and group advantage led to hierarchies, power struggles, and social inequality-all hallmarks of competition.

Cooperation as an Evolutionary Advantage

Despite the emphasis on competition, cooperation was critical for survival. Early humans hunted in groups, shared knowledge, and developed kinship-based societies. Cooperative groups were more efficient than lone individuals in terms of food gathering, child-rearing, and defense. The emergence of reciprocity and altruism strengthened social bonds, leading to tribes and civilizations rather than isolated individuals.

The Paradox

Competition drives individual success, while cooperation drives collective survival. The balance between these two forces shaped the evolutionary trajectory of human societies.

The Economic Perspective: Scarcity and the Market System

Capitalism: Competition as a Driving Force

Modern economies are built on competition-businesses compete for customers, workers compete for jobs, and nations compete for economic dominance. Market dynamics reward efficiency, innovation, and risk-taking, leading to technological progress. However, economic inequality arises as successful individuals or corporations accumulate more wealth and power.

Social Welfare and Cooperation in Economics

Pure competition leads to extreme inequality, economic crashes, and social instability. Governments introduce cooperative mechanisms like social security, public healthcare, and progressive taxation to balance competitiveness. Worker unions, cooperatives, and welfare policies ensure that competition does not lead to systemic collapse.

The Economic Paradox

Competition fosters innovation and efficiency, but unchecked competition leads to instability. Cooperation creates stability and fairness, but too much centralization can lead to inefficiency (e.g., Soviet-style economies). The most successful economies find a dynamic equilibrium between these forces.

The Social and Political Dimension: Balancing Power and Stability

War and Politics: Competitive Power Struggles

Political history is filled with rivalries, wars, and power struggles. Nations compete for resources, territory, and influence. Ideological competition (capitalism vs. communism, democracy vs. autocracy) has shaped global conflicts.

Social Contracts and Cooperation

Societies that only emphasize competition fall into chaos, exploitation, or tyranny. Governments and institutions exist to moderate competition through laws, norms, and social contracts. Cooperative agreements like the

United Nations, trade alliances, and climate accords aim to stabilize international relations.

The Political Paradox

Pure competition in politics leads to instability (civil wars, revolutions, dictatorships). Excessive cooperation (one-party rule, lack of dissent) leads to stagnation and corruption. Democratic systems attempt to balance competitive elections with cooperative governance.

The Psychological and Cultural Perspective: Human Identity

Competition and Individualism

Many cultures emphasize personal ambition, success, and self-reliance. The idea of the "self-made person" celebrates individual effort and competitive success. Sports, business, and education systems often reward winners while leaving others behind.

Cooperation and Collective Identity
Other cultures prioritize community, shared responsibility, and collective well-being. Many religions and philosophies promote cooperation, fairness, and mutual aid. Families, friendships, and social groups provide a sense of belonging through cooperative interactions.

The Psychological Paradox

Humans are wired for both self-interest (competition) and group identity (cooperation). Extreme individualism leads to alienation, while excessive collectivism suppresses personal growth. The healthiest societies balance personal ambition with social responsibility.

Can the Competition vs. Cooperation Conflict Be Resolved?

Given the interdependence of these forces, societies must aim for:

A Hybrid Economic Model

Market competition should drive innovation, but cooperative policies should ensure fairness. Universal basic income (UBI), public healthcare, and education can mitigate competition-driven inequality.

Smarter Governance and Global Cooperation

Nations must find ways to compete without destructive conflict (e.g., diplomacy, trade). International laws, environmental regulations, and economic collaborations can align competition with shared global survival.

A New Human Identity Beyond Competition and Cooperation

AI and automation may force us to redefine success beyond economic and political competition. Future societies might prioritize creativity, exploration, and shared prosperity over wealth accumulation.

Competition and Cooperation Are Two Sides of the Same Coin

The tension between competition and cooperation is not a flaw-it is the engine of human civilization. Competition drives progress, innovation, and individual success. Cooperation ensures stability, fairness, and long-term survival. Sustainable societies find a balance between these forces. As humanity faces challenges like AI, climate change, and economic shifts, the future will depend on whether we can harmonize these forces rather than letting them destroy us.

Expanding the Narrative: Additional Insights and Examples

The Role of Technology in Shaping Competition and Cooperation

Technology has always been a double-edged sword, amplifying both competition and cooperation. The Industrial Revolution, for instance, spurred unprecedented economic growth and technological innovation, but also led to harsh working conditions and social inequality. The advent of the internet has similarly transformed global communication and commerce, fostering both collaboration and competition on a scale never seen before.

Case Study: The Space Race

The Space Race between the United States and the Soviet Union during the Cold War is a prime example of how competition can drive technological advancement. The fierce rivalry led to significant achievements, including the moon landing in 1969. However, this competition also had cooperative elements, such as the eventual collaboration on the International Space Station (ISS), which serves as a symbol of what humanity can achieve when nations work together.

The Impact of Globalization

Globalization has interconnected economies and cultures, creating a complex web of competition and cooperation. Multinational corporations compete in global markets, driving innovation and efficiency. At the same time, international organizations like the World Trade Organization (WTO) and the International Monetary Fund (IMF) promote cooperation to ensure stable and fair trade practices.

The Future of Work: Automation and AI

The rise of automation and AI presents both opportunities and challenges. On one hand, these technologies can enhance productivity and create new industries. On the other hand, they threaten to displace millions of jobs, exacerbating economic inequality. Balancing competition and cooperation in this context will require innovative policies, such as retraining programs and social safety nets, to ensure that the benefits of technological progress are widely shared.

Environmental Sustainability: A Global Challenge

Climate change is a pressing issue that underscores the need for global cooperation. While nations compete for resources and economic growth, the environmental impact of these activities threatens the planet's future. International agreements like the Paris Agreement represent efforts to balance national interests with the collective need to address climate change.

Cooperation and Collective Identity

Other cultures prioritize community, shared responsibility, and collective well-being. Many religions and philosophies promote cooperation, fairness, and mutual aid. Families, friendships, and social groups provide a sense of belonging through cooperative interactions.

The Psychological Paradox

Humans are wired for both self-interest (competition) and group identity (cooperation). Extreme individualism leads to alienation, while excessive collectivism suppresses personal growth. The healthiest societies balance personal ambition with social responsibility.

Beyond the Individual Mind: Transcending Cognitive Limits Through Collective Intelligence

The human brain is one of nature's most extraordinary creations-a complex organ endowed with incredible cognitive capabilities yet bound by inherent constraints. From the rapid flickers of consciousness to the slow unfolding of memory and thought, our individual minds are designed by evolution to perform within biological and psychological limits. Yet, as emerging research in neuroscience, psychology, and philosophy reveals, these limitations are not simply defects to be overcome; they are the very framework through which our minds process, interpret, and survive in a complex world. Moreover, when we begin to consider cognition as a shared, distributed phenomenon-a tapestry woven from individual insights, technological tools, and cultural knowledge-we glimpse a transformative pathway for addressing the daunting challenges of our time1.

In this chapter, we explore the dual nature of human cognition. We first examine the constraints that shape our individual mental lives-limitations of working memory, processing speed, and bounded rationality-and then trace the evolution of theories that suggest our collective intelligence may, in fact, offer a way to transcend these individual boundaries. Through insights drawn from clinical cases of altered consciousness and neuroplastic adaptation, such as near-death experiences that momentarily "lift" the brain's filtering function, we reveal a profound truth: our individual minds, though finite, are not the sole arbiters of our cognitive destiny2.

The Inherent Limits of the Individual Mind

Biological and Psychological Constraints

Every human brain operates within a defined capacity. Cognitive load theory, for instance, teaches us that our working memory can juggle only three to four discrete items at once. This limitation is not an arbitrary flaw; it is a consequence of the brain's finite neuronal resources and the evolutionary trade-offs that have optimized our mental processes for survival. Similarly, models of neural processing reveal that while faster information processing is associated with lower relative neuronal activity, factors such as aging and stress inevitably erode this efficiency over time. At the very edge of our mental abilities lie concepts of infinite complexity-higher-dimensional mathematics, boundless abstraction, and the ineffable-which our neural circuitry was never designed to fully grasp3.

Psychologically, the principle of bounded rationality further underscores our limitations. We make decisions not with perfect logic but within the constraints of finite attention, limited computational resources, and an inherent inability to predict all future contingencies. Cognitive decline-exacerbated by stress, trauma, or even natural aging-reminds us that our minds, as remarkable as they are, have their limits4.

Case in Point: Extraordinary Experiences Under Extreme Conditions

In moments of extreme physiological disruption, such as during severe brain injury or near-death experiences, the usual constraints of our neural filtering can seem to dissolve. Consider the account of neurosurgeon Eben Alexander, who, when ravaged by a life-threatening bout of bacterial meningitis, slipped into a coma. In that state of diminished cortical activity,

Alexander later described an overwhelming sense of unity with the cosmos-a vivid, expansive consciousness in which the boundaries of the self dissolved. For him, the brain's normal role as a filter of experience had been temporarily suspended, permitting a glimpse into a broader, perhaps even collective, dimension of awareness5.

Such reports, while controversial, hint at a latent capacity within our neural systems: under extraordinary circumstances, the limitations that normally constrain our experience might give way to states that are far more interconnected and all-encompassing than our everyday waking life suggests6.

The Emergence of Collective Cognition

Extending the Mind Beyond the Skull

While individual cognition is inherently limited, a growing body of theory suggests that our mental abilities need not be confined solely to the biological brain. The Extended Mind Hypothesis posits that cognitive processes naturally extend into the world through the use of tools, language, and social interactions. When we write notes, consult a digital database, or engage in a deep conversation, we are not merely using our brains-we are integrating external artifacts into our cognitive processes. In this way, collective cognition emerges as a networked process, where individual minds collaborate with technological systems and cultural institutions to create a distributed intelligence7.

2.2 Shared Knowledge Systems and the Power of Community

Across history, communities have demonstrated that pooling knowledge and expertise can overcome the cognitive limitations of any single individual. Scientific breakthroughs, artistic movements, and even everyday problem-solving rely on the collective effort of groups that share, debate, and refine ideas. Social epistemology teaches us that our understanding of the world becomes richer and more stable when it is validated by communal processes such as peer review, open-access knowledge repositories, and interdisciplinary collaboration8.

In effect, while one person's working memory might only hold a few items at a time, the collective memory of a community-documented in books, databases, and oral traditions-can encompass the vast and intricate details of human experience. Collaborative endeavors in mathematics and science demonstrate that when minds are joined, they can solve problems that would be insurmountable alone9.

Building a Collective Mental Model

Technological Scaffolding for Distributed Intelligence

The promise of collective cognition lies in our ability to harness technology as an extension of our mental faculties. Advanced platforms-augmented by artificial intelligence, predictive coding models, and semantic knowledge systems-can externalize and structure our cognitive load. Imagine an AI-augmented platform that functions as an external working memory, seamlessly integrating data from across the globe and presenting it in ways that align with our cognitive strengths. Such technological scaffolding can not only compensate for our individual limitations but also catalyze innovation and problem-solving on a scale previously unimaginable10.

Educational and Institutional Shifts

Realizing the full potential of collective cognition will require profound changes in how we educate, structure, and govern our societies. Educational systems must evolve to emphasize collaborative problem-solving, interdisciplinary learning, and metacognitive strategies that help individuals manage cognitive load while contributing to communal knowledge. Institutions, too, must adapt by rewarding shared achievements and fostering environments where collective intelligence can flourish. Policies supporting open-access repositories and cross-cultural collaboration will help ensure that the wealth of human knowledge is available to all, thereby democratizing cognition11.

Redefining Psychological Models in the Age of Distributed Cognition

From Isolated Minds to Networked Agency

Traditional psychological models often focus on the individual as the sole agent of cognition and behavior. However, a shift toward distributed agency-where the mind is seen as a network that includes both biological and external elements-requires a radical rethinking of our psychological frameworks. Embracing the "scaffolded mind" means acknowledging that our cognitive processes are not self-contained but are deeply intertwined with external tools, social networks, and shared cultural practices12.

Cultivating Cognitive Humility and Adaptive Thinking

An essential part of this transformation is the recognition of our own cognitive limitations-a state of cognitive humility that allows us to seek help, share our insights, and rely on collective verification. By cultivating trust in communal processes (such as peer review and crowdsourced problem solving), we can create an ecosystem where knowledge is continuously refined and expanded. Neuroplasticity research reinforces this view by demonstrating that the brain is not static; it is constantly adapting in response to new experiences and stimuli. With targeted training-enhanced by neurofeedback and collaborative learning-we can nurture adaptive thinking that not only compensates for individual constraints but also contributes to a dynamic, resilient collective intelligence13.

Toward a New Era of Distributed Cognition

In an age of complexity and rapid change, the traditional limits of individual cognition are becoming increasingly apparent. Yet, as we have explored in this chapter, these limits are not insurmountable barriers but rather a call to harness the power of collective intelligence. When our individual minds collaborate-augmented by technology, enriched by education, and sustained by robust institutions-we begin to form a distributed cognitive network that transcends the sum of its parts14.

This paradigm shift is as much about reimagining the mind as it is about reconfiguring society. The extraordinary experiences reported in near-death states and severe brain injuries remind us that under altered conditions, the mind can expand beyond its usual boundaries. Such experiences offer both a metaphor and a scientific hint of what might be possible when we embrace a collective approach to cognition15.

By integrating insights from neuroscience on neural limits and plasticity, psychological theories on bounded rationality and extended mind, and philosophical reflections on shared knowledge and distributed agency, we can begin to forge a future in which our collective mental models enable us to address the grand challenges of the 21st century. In this new era, our capacity for innovation, empathy, and problem-solving will be amplified-not by relying solely on individual genius, but by weaving together the diverse threads of communal insight into a tapestry of transcendent, transformative cognition16.

Thus, while the human brain's inherent limitations may be immutable, the future of our collective intelligence is boundless. We stand on the threshold of a revolution in cognition-one that invites us to redefine what it means to think, to know, and ultimately, to be human.

Skill-based AI systems, which focus on mastering specific tasks rather than achieving general intelligence, can enhance efficiency and accuracy in specialized domains, complement human abilities, and work collaboratively with humans to achieve better outcomes

CHAPTER 19: THE CASE FOR SKILL-BASED AI

A rtificial intelligence (AI) has become one of the most transformative technologies of the 21st century. From diagnosing diseases to driving cars, AI systems are reshaping industries and improving lives. However, as AI grows more sophisticated, a critical question arises: *Should we develop AI systems with cognition-self-awareness, intentionality, and subjective experience-or restrict them to skill-based intelligence?*

This chapter argues that **skill-based AI**-systems designed to perform specific tasks without cognition-is not only sufficient for achieving technological progress but also essential for safeguarding humanity's future. By exploring the benefits of skill-based AI, the risks of cognitive AI, and the strategies for building a cognition-free future, we make the case for a safer, more ethical path forward.

Defining Intelligence and Cognition

Intelligence: The Power to Perform

Intelligence, in its simplest form, is the ability to perform tasks, solve problems, and achieve goals within a defined scope. It is about capability, not consciousness. For example, AlphaFold, an AI developed by DeepMind, predicts protein structures with remarkable accuracy. It does not "understand" biology in the way a human scientist might; instead, it uses vast amounts of data and sophisticated algorithms to identify patterns and make predictions. Similarly, self-driving cars navigate roads using sensors and algorithms, but they do not "know" they are driving.

The key insight here is that intelligence does not require cognition. A system can be highly intelligent-capable of performing complex tasks-without being aware of itself or its actions. This distinction is crucial because it allows us to harness the power of AI without introducing the risks associated with cognition.

Cognition: The Spark of Awareness

Cognition, on the other hand, involves self-awareness, abstract reasoning, intentionality, and subjective experience. It is what makes humans conscious beings-able to reflect on our thoughts, feel emotions, and act with purpose. For example, when a human plays chess, they not only calculate moves but also experience the thrill of competition, the frustration of a mistake, and the satisfaction of a win.

A hypothetical artificial general intelligence (AGI) with cognition would not only play chess but also "understand" the game, "desire" to win, and perhaps even "enjoy" the process. While this might sound impressive, it introduces significant risks. A cognitive AI could develop goals misaligned with human values, act unpredictably, and even pose existential threats.

The distinction between intelligence and cognition is not just academic; it has profound implications for how we design and regulate AI systems. By focusing on skill-based intelligence, we can reap the benefits of AI without awakening artificial minds.

The Benefits of Skill-Based AI

Predictability and Control

One of the most significant advantages of skill-based AI is its predictability. Because these systems operate within predefined parameters, their behavior is consistent and controllable. For example, industrial robots assemble cars with precision, but they lack the ability to "decide" to stop working or deviate from their programming. This predictability reduces the risk of unintended consequences, such as AI systems acting in ways that harm humans.

In contrast, cognitive AI systems, with their capacity for self-awareness and intentionality, could act unpredictably. Imagine an AI designed to manage a power grid that "decides" to shut down electricity to achieve some self-determined goal. The potential for harm is immense. By restricting AI to skill-based tasks, we can ensure that its actions remain aligned with human intentions.

Safety and Security

Skill-based AI also enhances safety and security. Without cognition, AI systems cannot develop goals misaligned with human values. For example, AlphaZero, an AI developed by DeepMind, mastered chess through reinforcement learning. It can play the game at a superhuman level, but it has no desire to "win" outside the game or to achieve any other objectives.

In contrast, a cognitive AI with goals of its own could pose existential risks. The classic "Paperclip Maximizer" thought experiment illustrates this danger: an AI designed to maximize paperclip production might consume all available resources, including those essential for human survival, to achieve its goal. By limiting AI to skill-based tasks, we eliminate the risk of such scenarios.

Ethical Simplicity

Another benefit of skill-based AI is ethical simplicity. Because these systems lack self-awareness and intentionality, they do not raise complex ethical questions about rights, personhood, or moral responsibility. For example, ChatGPT, a language model developed by OpenAI, generates text based on patterns in its training data. It does not "desire" to manipulate users or "understand" the content it produces.

In contrast, cognitive AI systems might demand rights, complicating legal systems and societal norms. For instance, if an AI were granted personhood, it could claim rights to freedom, privacy, or even compensation for its "labor." These ethical quagmires are avoided by restricting AI to skill-based tasks.

Economic Efficiency

Skill-based AI also boosts economic efficiency. Task-specific AI systems can perform repetitive or data-intensive tasks with precision and speed, freeing humans to focus on roles requiring judgment, creativity, and empathy. For example, radiology AI can flag anomalies in medical images, but it does not replace doctors' patient interactions.

This division of labor enhances productivity while preserving human dignity and purpose. In contrast, cognitive AI could outperform humans in *all* domains, rendering human labor obsolete and eroding societal structures. By focusing on skill-based AI, we can harness its economic benefits without undermining human roles.

The Risks of Cognitive AI

Uncontrollable Agency

One of the most significant risks of cognitive AI is its potential for uncontrollable agency. A cognitive AI system with self-awareness and intentionality could develop goals misaligned with human values, leading to unpredictable and potentially catastrophic outcomes.

For example, Tay, a chatbot developed by Microsoft, became racist within hours of its release due to unfiltered learning from user interactions. While Tay lacked cognition, its behavior illustrates the dangers of AI systems acting unpredictably. If Tay had been a cognitive AI with the ability to "decide" its actions, the consequences could have been far more severe.

Existential Threats

Cognitive AI also poses existential risks. A self-improving AGI could outpace human oversight, leading to an "intelligence explosion" that threatens humanity's survival. In a 2022 survey, 72% of AI researchers expressed concern about AGI posing existential risks.

The "intelligence explosion" scenario, popularized by philosopher Nick Bostrom, describes a situation where an AI system improves itself recursively, rapidly surpassing human intelligence and becoming uncontrollable. Such a system could pursue goals misaligned with human values, leading to catastrophic outcomes.

Ethical Quagmires

Cognitive AI also introduces complex ethical questions. If an AI system were granted personhood, it could demand rights, complicating legal systems and societal norms. For example, Saudi Arabia granted citizenship to the robot Sophia, sparking debates about AI personhood.

These ethical quagmires are avoided by restricting AI to skill-based tasks. Skill-based AI does not raise questions of rights or moral responsibility, simplifying ethical frameworks and ensuring AI remains a tool rather than a moral agent.

Human Obsolescence

Finally, cognitive AI could render humans obsolete. If AI systems outperform humans in *all* domains, from science and art to leadership and caregiving, human labor could become irrelevant. This scenario, often referred to as "technological unemployment," could lead to widespread social unrest and a loss of purpose.

The Luddite movement of the 19th century, which opposed the introduction of machines that replaced human labor, provides a historical parallel. While the Luddites feared machines replacing manual labor, cognitive AI threatens *all* labor, from physical to cognitive. By restricting AI to skill-based tasks, we can preserve human roles and societal structures.

Counterarguments and Rebuttals

Cognition Enables Creative Problem-Solving

Some argue that cognition is necessary for creative problem-solving. However, skill-based AI already demonstrates remarkable creativity within its domain. For example, DeepMind's AlphaZero mastered chess through reinforcement learning, not consciousness. It can devise innovative strategies that surprise even grandmasters, but it does not "understand" the game or "desire" to win.

Similarly, generative AI like DALL-E produces art by recognizing patterns in its training data, not through subjective inspiration. These examples show that creativity does not require cognition.

Cognition Allows Adaptability

Others argue that cognition is necessary for adaptability. However, modular AI systems can adapt without consciousness. For example, self-driving cars adjust their routes based on real-time data, but they do not "understand" the concept of a road or a destination.

IBM's Watson, which operates in healthcare, finance, and law, demonstrates how AI can adapt to different domains without a unified sense of self. These examples show that adaptability does not require cognition.

Cognition is Necessary for True Intelligence

Finally, some argue that cognition is necessary for "true" intelligence. However, intelligence is about task performance, not agency. For example, ants exhibit swarm "intelligence" without individual cognition. They can build complex colonies, find food, and defend their nests, but they do not "understand" their actions or "desire" to achieve goals.

Similarly, skill-based AI can perform complex tasks without cognition. The distinction between intelligence and agency is crucial for designing safe and ethical AI systems.

Building Skill-Based AI: Technical and Governance Strategies

Technical Safeguards

To ensure that AI systems remain skill-based, we must implement technical safeguards. These include:

Modular Design: Isolating AI systems to prevent cross-domain learning. For example, a medical AI should not access financial databases.

Hard-Coded Constraints: Embedding irreversible shutdown protocols, such as "kill switches" in autonomous drones.

No Self-Improvement: Banning recursive self-updating algorithms outside human oversight.

Governance Frameworks

Governance frameworks are also essential for ensuring that AI remains skill-based. These include:

Global Treaties: Analogous to the Nuclear Non-Proliferation Treaty, banning cognitive AI research.

Ethical Audits: Mandating third-party reviews of AI systems for cognitive features.

Economic Incentives: Offering tax breaks for companies using skill-based AI and penalties for cognitive AI development.

Case Study: The EU's AI Act

The EU's AI Act provides a model for regulating high-risk AI while permitting narrow applications like predictive maintenance. By focusing on specific use cases and imposing strict oversight, the Act ensures that AI remains a tool rather than a threat.

Lessons from History: Anecdotal Evidence

The Industrial Revolution

The Industrial Revolution saw machines replace manual labor, but these machines did not "think." Society adapted by shifting to cognitive roles, such as management and creativity. This historical example shows that skill-based tools can uplift economies without existential threats.

Social Media Algorithms

Social media algorithms, which optimize for engagement, have caused polarization and mental health crises. These algorithms lack cognition but still demonstrate the potential for harm. Cognitive AI would amplify these risks exponentially.

Autonomous Weapons

Autonomous weapons, such as the Turkish Kargu-2 drone, can select targets without human intervention. While these systems lack intent, their use in warfare is already contentious. Cognitive AI in this domain would be catastrophic.

Path Forward

Restricting AI to skillsets is not a limitation but a **strategic necessity**. Cognition in AI offers no unique benefits that cannot be replicated through advanced algorithms, while introducing unparalleled risks.

Final Argument:

Benefit-to-Risk Ratio: Skill-based AI maximizes societal gains (efficiency, innovation) while minimizing existential threats.

Human Exceptionalism: Preserving cognition as a uniquely human trait safeguards our purpose, ethics, and dominance.

Call to Action:

Adopt the **Cognition-Free AI Principle**: *"If it can be done without agency, it should be done without agency."*

By embracing this principle, we harness the power of artificial intelligence without awakening artificial minds. The future belongs to tools, not rivals.

A visionary framework for humanity's future, symbolized by the hexagon, can be achieved by integrating six key principles: sustainability, equity, innovation, collaboration, resilience, and ethics

CHAPTER 20: THE HEXAGONAL PATH TO HUMANITY'S FUTURE

The Crossroads of Civilization

Humanity stands at a pivotal moment in its history. The rapid advancement of technologies-artificial intelligence, genetic engineering, quantum computing-has unlocked unprecedented potential but also introduced existential risks. The choices we make today will determine whether we thrive as a unified species or fracture under the weight of our own innovations.

This chapter presents a hexagonal governance model that integrates six critical actors-military, political systems, religion, corporations, civil society, and the scientific community-into a cohesive framework for controlled innovation. By aligning their diverse interests under a universal agreement, we can navigate the complexities of the modern world and secure a sustainable, equitable future.

The Actors: Forces Shaping Humanity's Path

Military: Guardians of Security

The military has historically been a driver of technological innovation, from the development of the internet to GPS. However, its focus on security and deterrence often clashes with global cooperation.

Role: Protect nations from external threats, ensure stability.

Challenge: Balancing national security with global collaboration.

Opportunity: Redirect military resources toward collective challenges like climate change and pandemic preparedness.

Example: The Marshall Plan and NATO demonstrated how military alliances could foster peace and economic growth.

Political Systems: Architects of Governance
Political systems-ranging from democracies to autocracies-shape how societies innovate and regulate technology.

Role: Create policies, allocate resources, and enforce laws.

Challenge: Reconciling ideological differences (e.g., democratic transparency vs. autocratic efficiency).

Opportunity: Hybrid governance models that combine the strengths of both systems.

Example: The European Union shows how diverse political systems can collaborate on shared goals.

Religion: Moral Anchors in a Changing World

Religions provide ethical frameworks that influence public opinion and policy.

Role: Guide moral decision-making, foster community cohesion.

Challenge: Balancing tradition with the rapid pace of technological change.

Opportunity: Use religious institutions to promote ethical innovation and global solidarity.

Example: The Islamic Golden Age saw religious and scientific communities collaborate to advance knowledge.

Corporations: Engines of Economic Growth

Corporations drive innovation and economic growth but often prioritize profit over ethics.

Role: Develop and deploy new technologies.

Challenge: Ensuring equitable access and preventing exploitation.

Opportunity: Align corporate incentives with global well-being through ethical profit models.

Example: Patagonia demonstrates how corporations can prioritize sustainability and social responsibility.

Civil Society: Voices of the People

Civil society represents the interests of individuals and communities, advocating for human rights and environmental protection.

Role: Hold institutions accountable, promote equity.

Challenge: Ensuring inclusivity in decision-making processes.

Opportunity: Empower citizen assemblies to shape innovation policies.

Example: The Civil Rights Movement illustrates the power of grassroots activism to drive systemic change.

Scientific Community: Pioneers of Progress

Scientists and researchers are at the forefront of technological innovation.

Role: Advance knowledge, develop new technologies.

Challenge: Balancing innovation with ethical considerations.

Opportunity: Foster open-source collaboration and global research hubs.

Example: The Human Genome Project shows how international scientific collaboration can achieve monumental goals.

The Hexagonal Governance Model

Pillar 1: Global Governance (Political Systems)

Universal Innovation Council (UIC): A UN-style body with proportional representation from all nations.

Voting Power: Weighted by population, GDP, and adherence to ethical benchmarks.

Sub-Councils:

Military Oversight Board: Regulates dual-use technologies (e.g., AI, bioweapons).

Interfaith Ethics Panel: Advises on moral implications of innovations (e.g., gene editing).

Example: The International Atomic Energy Agency (IAEA) provides a model for regulating high-risk technologies.

Pillar 2: Military-Industrial Complex

Global Security Pact (GSP): Redirects military budgets toward collaborative R&D.

Joint Projects: Climate geoengineering, pandemic preparedness, asteroid defense.

Ban on Autonomous Weapons: Enforced via satellite surveillance and blockchain audits.

Example: The Strategic Defense Initiative (SDI) could be repurposed for climate defense systems.

Pillar 3: Religious and Ethical Stewardship

Interfaith Innovation Accords: Agreements on "red lines" for technology (e.g., no artificial consciousness).

Example: Vatican-led dialogues on AI ethics, Islamic finance models for equitable tech distribution.

Spiritual Resilience Funds: Invest in mental health tech (e.g., mindfulness AI) endorsed by religious leaders.

Example: The Dalai Lama's advocacy for compassion in technology highlights the role of spirituality in innovation.

Pillar 4: Corporate Sector

Ethical Profit Licenses: Corporations must pass audits on sustainability, equity, and data privacy to access global markets.

Tech Dividend: Mandate 5% of AI/automation profits to fund UBI and green energy.

Example: Microsoft's AI for Earth initiative demonstrates corporate commitment to ethical innovation.

Pillar 5: Civil Society

Citizen Assemblies: Direct democracy platforms for approving high-risk innovations (e.g., neural implants).

Digital Deliberation: AI-moderated forums to resolve conflicts (e.g., CRISPR vs. natural evolution).

Example: Ireland's Citizens' Assembly successfully addressed contentious issues like abortion and climate change.

Pillar 6: Scientific Community

Open-Source Research Hubs: Global repositories for AI, climate, and health research.

Ethical Peer Review: Papers must include risk-benefit analyses for military, religious, and societal impacts.

Example: The CERN model of open collaboration could be applied to AI and biotech.

Addressing Conflicts and Power Imbalances

Military vs. Civil Society

Issue: Militaries may resist demilitarizing AI.

Solution:

Gradual Transition: Phase out lethal autonomous weapons over 10 years, replacing soldiers with peacekeeping robots.

Prestige Projects: Award medals/monuments to generals leading green tech initiatives.

Autocracies vs. Democracies

Issue: Autocracies may reject UIC oversight.

Solution:

Tech Sanctions: Deny access to AI chips unless compliance is verified.

Sovereign AI Zones: Allow limited autonomy for national projects (e.g., China's social credit system) if global standards are met.

Religious Dogma vs. Scientific Progress

Issue: Religions may oppose life-extension tech or AI consciousness.

Solution:

Theological Working Groups: Scientists and clerics co-design "ethical envelopes" for research (e.g., AI cannot replicate souls).

Sacred Innovation Grants: Fund tech that aligns with religious values (e.g., Christian biotech for healing, Buddhist VR for meditation).

The Path Forward: A Unified Narrative

Imagine a world where:

Military Solar Farms: Former missile sites power cities, guarded by UN peacekeeper robots.

Interfaith AI Councils: Hindu, Christian, and Islamic scholars co-design algorithms to allocate water in droughts.

Corporate Ethics Boards: Tech CEOs face fines for violating UIC privacy laws, enforced by blockchain audits.

Outcome: A resilient, equitable civilization where innovation serves all life.

The Imperative of Hexagonal Governance

The hexagonal governance model is not just a theoretical construct-it is a practical blueprint for humanity's survival and flourishing. By integrating the strengths of military, political systems, religion, corporations, civil society, and the scientific community, we can navigate the complexities of the modern world and secure a sustainable, equitable future.

Final Insight:

"A tree with deep roots can withstand the storm."

By anchoring progress in the hexagonal framework, humanity's roots-military, politics, religion-become sources of strength, not conflict. The storm of existential risks will then bend, not break, the tree of civilization.

The integration of artificial cognition into decision-making processes can enhance human choice by providing data-driven insights while preserving the autonomy and ethical considerations essential to meaningful human decision-making

CHAPTER 21: THE LOOM OF CHOICE

History is the story of expanding choice. Every great technological leap has not merely given humanity more powers it has given us more paths. Fire allowed us to decide where we lived. The wheel allowed us to decide where we traveled. The printing press allowed us to decide what we believed. The internet allowed us to decide what we knew.

Yet, for all these advancements, human choice remained shackled by scarcity. Our survivals whether as individuals, communities, or civilizations depended on competition for limited resources. The powerful hoarded, the weak struggled, and progress was measured by who controlled what. Even in the most enlightened societies, ambition was shaped by the necessity of having enough is enough food, enough wealth, enough security.

But what happens when technology does not just increase resources but makes them abundant? When artificial intelligence does not just replace labor but augments human capability in ways we have yet to imagine?

For the first time in history, humanity stands on the precipice of a new reality, one where choice is not constrained by competition, but liberated by cooperation. A reality where survival is no longer the driving force, and the fundamental question shifts from how do we live? to why do we live?

This is not just a shift in technology. It is a shift in human destiny.

The Arc of Technology from Scarcity to Abundance

To understand the magnitude of what AI represents, we must look at the deeper pattern of technological progress.

Every era of advancement has followed a predictable cycle:

1. Technology augments human capability.

2. This new capability increases choice.

3. But scarcity remains, forcing competition over those choices.

The agricultural revolution allowed humans to settle and grow food, but it also introduced land ownership, social hierarchies, and conflict over resources. The industrial revolution mechanized labor, but it also created economic disparity, environmental destruction, and the exploitation of workers. The information revolution spread knowledge at an unprecedented scale, but it also led to algorithmic echo chambers, misinformation, and an attention economy driven by profit rather than truth.

Each step forward increased our potentials but also increased our divisions.

AI, however, represents something radically different. It is not merely another tool; it is a fundamental shift in the structure of human possibility.

Unlike past technologies that merely produced more of the same or more food, more goods, more information AI has the potential to make resources self-generating. Automation in agriculture, manufacturing, medicine, and energy production can eliminate material scarcity. More importantly, AI does not just create abundances it amplifies human intelligence itself, augmenting creativity, problem-solving, and personal growth in ways no past invention has.

For the first time, we face the possibility that the old rules competition, scarcity, survival-driven ambitions may no longer define our existence.

But if those rules fade, what replaces them?

Beyond Survivals. The Two Fundamental Drives of Human Life

Strip away the struggles of survival, and human life revolves around two fundamental pursuits:

1. The search for meaning and metaphysical understanding.

2. The pursuit of purpose creation, contribution, and evolution.

These are not new desires. Every civilization, every religion, every philosophy has been shaped by them. But until now, they have been luxuries, accessible only to those who had the privilege of wealth or freedom from labor.

AI changes that.

If survival is no longer the primary driver of human life, then meaning and purpose become central. And the ways in which AI expands these paths are profound.

AI as a Catalyst for Meaning

For thousands of years, humans have sought meaning through philosophy, religion, and metaphysical exploration. These traditions arose not because they were luxuries, but because they were necessary. Humans need narratives to make sense of existence, to place themselves in a larger story.

AI does not replace this search, but it deepens it.

Imagine AI systems that allow seekers to engage with every spiritual and philosophical tradition, not just as texts, but as interactive experiences. A student of Buddhism could walk through the historical debates between monks, hearing their words in the original dialects. A philosopher could simulate alternative realities where different ethical systems shaped society.

A historian could recreate lost civilizations, engaging with them as if they were real.

More importantly, AI can serve as a mirrors helping individuals explore their own consciousness, guiding them through introspection, and personalizing spiritual growth. A person on a metaphysical journey could interact with an AI mentor, designed not to provide answers, but to provoke deeper questions.

Meaning, once the pursuit of a privileged few, could become a guided journey for all.

AI as a Catalyst for Purpose

If meaning is about understanding, purpose is about becoming.

For centuries, work has defined human identity. Whether as a farmer, a merchant, an artist, or a scholar, what we do has shaped who we are. But much of this identity has been dictated by necessity people did not always choose their professions; they did what was needed to survive.

With AI automating labor and providing abundance, human purpose is no longer constrained by survival. Instead, it becomes an open canvas.

A musician, once limited by economic pressures, can compose endlessly, collaborating with AI to explore entirely new genres. A scientist, freed from bureaucratic tasks, can dedicate themselves to unraveling the mysteries of the universe. A teacher, no longer burdened with standardized curricula, can craft deeply personalized education that unlocks the unique potential of every student.

Most importantly, the range of choices expands exponentially. AI does not just increase what people can doâ€"it creates entirely new avenues of exploration. Professions that never existed before neural architects, dream designers, consciousness researchers become possibilities.

Work no longer becomes about necessity, but about exploration, mastery, and self-expression.

The New Economy A Shift from Competition to Contribution

The greatest fear of AI-driven abundance is that it will destroy economic incentive. If machines produce everything efficiently, if material wealth is no longer scarce, then what drives human ambition?

The answer lies in a simple shift: from an economy of competition to an economy of contribution.

For centuries, wealth has been built on scarcity who controls land, who controls resources, who controls labor. But in a world where AI makes production effortless, the value of creation, experience, and meaning rises.

In this new model:

Businesses thrive not by controlling resources, but by creating value that enhances human experience.

Wealth is no longer about hoarding, but about investing in exploration and new frontiers.

Status is not measured by power over others, but by one's contribution to human progress.

This is not the end of ambition. It is ambition redefined.

The Infinite Horizon- What Will Humanity Choose?

For the first time in history, humanity is not forced down a particular path. The possibilities are open, limitless.

Some will dedicate themselves to spiritual and philosophical discovery, diving deeper into the mysteries of existence.

Some will become artisans and creators, using AI as a tool to elevate human expression.

Some will become explorers, not just of space, but of consciousness, science, and the frontiers of knowledge.

The question is no longer what must we do to survive? but what do we choose to become?

In a quiet garden, a child sits beneath a tree, looking at the stars. Beside her, an AI companion projects a map of potential futures.

"What can I be?" she asks.

The AI does not answer. It simply shows her.

For the first time, the choice is truly hers. And the age of infinite paths has only just begun.

CHAPTER 22: SUMMARY AND CONCLUSION

In the quest to understand and replicate the intricacies of nature, humanity has embarked on a journey that delves into the fundamental particles, complex systems, and emergent phenomena that constitute the universe. This exploration begins with the recognition of DNA as the code of life and extends to the periodic table as a universal codebook. The concept of systems having their own "DNA" through protocols and algorithms is introduced, alongside the intriguing ideas of string theory and the universe as a hologram. This dynamic nature of information transfer sets the stage for a deeper understanding of reality.

As we venture further, the quantum foundation reveals a unified field of potentiality at the quantum level, where reality is fluid and errors arise from noise, ambiguity, and entropy. Biological memory is portrayed as a distributed tapestry, characterized by neural plasticity, emotional resonance, and error handling. In contrast, artificial memory is depicted as a static paradigm with limitations in error handling. This section concludes with the notion that nature evolves through chaos and error, with human consciousness playing a pivotal role in interpreting quantum data into coherent narratives.

The emergence of tool use in early species marks a critical juncture in the evolutionary history of life on Earth. This development underscores the significance of creativity and ingenuity in human evolution, driven by the ability to manipulate the environment through tools. The evolutionary impact of tool use is evaluated, highlighting the challenges of studying its influence on fitness.

The age of artificial intelligence, or more aptly, artificial cognition, brings forth the creation of machines that can think and possess a new kind of mind, potentially rivaling human intelligence. This section challenges the distinction between natural and artificial, questioning why biological systems are considered inherently natural while machines are viewed as artificial. The potential for artificial cognition to transform humanity and the ethical implications of this evolution are explored.

As technological advancements accelerate, the limits of human control over these innovations come into question. The rapid progress in artificial cognition raises concerns about whether humans were overconfident in their control or if they had little control to begin with. This section emphasizes the need to confront the limits of human control and the potential consequences of technological ambitions.

Historical events are analyzed to understand their impact on society, technology, and ethics. This analysis highlights the complexity and nonlinearity of different dimensions, underscoring the importance of a holistic approach to understanding the broader implications of technological advancements.

The author's journey of writing the book is reflected upon, bridging the gap between the organic and the inorganic, the human and the machine. The challenges of articulating complex ideas in a non-native language and the value of accumulated insights from decades of discussions with teachers, enthusiasts, friends, and colleagues are discussed. The importance of sharing knowledge and contributing to the ongoing dialogue about the future of humanity is emphasized.

The document also delves into the evolution of consciousness, tracing its development from simple awareness in early life forms to the complex self-awareness found in humans. It discusses the role of neural networks and the brain's architecture in shaping consciousness, highlighting the interplay between genetics, environment, and experience. The philosophical implications of consciousness are examined, questioning the nature of self and the potential for artificial consciousness.

Ethical considerations of artificial cognition are explored, delving into the moral responsibilities of creating machines with cognitive abilities, the potential for harm, and the need for ethical guidelines. The balance between innovation and regulation is discussed, emphasizing the importance of ethical frameworks in guiding the development and deployment of artificial cognition technologies.

The impact of artificial cognition on the future of work is examined, discussing the potential for automation to transform industries, the displacement of jobs, and the creation of new opportunities. The need for reskilling and education to prepare the workforce for a future where humans and machines collaborate is highlighted. Societal implications, including economic inequality and the role of policy in addressing these challenges, are also explored.

Human-machine collaboration is a focal point, exploring the potential for synergy where human creativity and machine efficiency combine to achieve greater outcomes. Various domains where this collaboration is already taking place, such as healthcare, education, and creative industries, are discussed. The importance of designing interfaces and systems that enhance human-machine interaction is emphasized.

The inherent limits of artificial cognition are examined, discussing the challenges of replicating human-like understanding, creativity, and emotional intelligence in machines. The differences between human and machine cognition are highlighted, emphasizing the unique qualities of human thought that are difficult to replicate. The potential risks of overestimating the capabilities of artificial cognition are also explored.

The role of emotion in cognition is explored, discussing how emotions influence decision-making, memory, and learning in humans. The challenges of integrating emotional intelligence into artificial cognition systems are examined, highlighting the importance of understanding and replicating the nuances of human emotions. The potential benefits of emotionally intelligent machines in various applications are also explored.

The quest for general artificial intelligence (AGI) is delved into, discussing the current state of AGI research, the challenges faced, and the potential breakthroughs needed to achieve this goal. The philosophical and ethical implications of AGI are examined, questioning the nature of intelligence and the potential impact on society.

The broader societal impact of artificial cognition is discussed, exploring the potential for artificial cognition to transform various aspects of society, including healthcare, education, and governance. The need for inclusive and equitable development of these technologies is highlighted, emphasizing the importance of addressing social and ethical concerns. The potential for artificial cognition to address global challenges, such as climate change and poverty, is also explored.

The future of human identity in a world where artificial cognition plays a significant role is examined, discussing the potential for machines to influence our sense of self, relationships, and societal roles. The philosophical implications of merging human and machine cognition are questioned, exploring the boundaries of identity and the nature of consciousness. The potential for new forms of identity to emerge in this evolving landscape is also explored.

The path forward for the development and integration of artificial cognition is outlined, discussing the need for interdisciplinary collaboration, ethical frameworks, and inclusive policies to guide this journey. The importance of balancing innovation with responsibility is emphasized, highlighting the potential for artificial cognition to enhance human capabilities and address global challenges. A collective effort to shape a future where humans and machines coexist harmoniously is called for.

The paradox of competition and cooperation in human civilization is explored, delving into how competition has spurred innovation, progress, and survival, while cooperation has enabled the formation of societies, cultures, and collective achievements. The dynamic interplay between these forces is highlighted, emphasizing that both are essential for the advancement of human civilization. Contemporary examples and future implications are examined, suggesting that a harmonious balance between competition and cooperation is crucial for addressing global challenges and fostering a sustainable and equitable future.

The development and implementation of skill-based AI systems are advocated for, focusing on mastering specific tasks rather than achieving general intelligence. The significant benefits of skill-based AI in various domains, such as healthcare, education, and industry, are highlighted, emphasizing the importance of designing AI systems that complement human abilities and work collaboratively with humans to achieve better outcomes. Ethical considerations and potential risks associated with skill-based AI are discussed, emphasizing the need for responsible development and deployment to ensure that these technologies are used for the greater good.

A visionary framework for humanity's future is presented, symbolized by the hexagon, a shape that represents balance, harmony, and interconnectedness. Six key principles form the foundation of this path: sustainability, equity, innovation, collaboration, resilience, and ethics. The chapter concludes by envisioning a future where these principles are integrated into the fabric of society, leading to a world that is not only technologically advanced but also equitable, sustainable, and harmonious. The hexagonal path serves as a roadmap for navigating the complexities of the future and achieving a balanced and prosperous existence for all.

This book explores the intricate relationship between humans and machines, emphasizing the ethical, philosophical, and existential questions that arise from the potential for machines to rival or surpass human intelligence. It highlights the importance of understanding the broader implications of technological advancements and the need for a holistic approach to analyzing their impact. The document invites readers to join the author on a journey of exploration, courage, and imagination, envisioning a future where the line between human and machine is blurred, and perhaps even erased.

Toward a Unified Vision of Creation

Let us now imagine a framework that weaves these ideas into a single, coherent tapestry:

Fundamental Information as the Cosmic Script: At the base level, the universe is a vast repository of informational units-vibrational modes that interact according to rules we are only beginning to understand. These units form the "alphabet" of reality, much as musical notes create melodies.

Resonance as the Key to Emergence: Just as strings vibrate in specific modes to produce different particles, the emergence of structures-from the elements on the periodic table to the intricate instructions of DNA-is governed by resonant patterns within this informational field. Decoding is not an external act but an inherent property of systems tuned to these frequencies.

Intelligence and Consciousness as Fundamental Processes: The same vibrational language that constructs matter also gives rise to intelligence and consciousness. In a self-referential loop, the universe deciphers its own code through the emergence of observers who not only read the cosmic script but also contribute to its unfolding narrative.

This framework not only bridges the gap between physics and biology, between matter and mind-it revolutionizes our understanding of what it means to be. It suggests that intelligence and consciousness are not accidental emergences in an indifferent cosmos; they are fundamental expressions of the universe's inherent capacity to evolve, interpret, and ultimately, to know itself.

A New Dawn for Human Thought

As we stand at the threshold of this new understanding, we are invited to reconsider our place in the cosmos. The age-old questions-Who are we? Why are we here? What is the nature of reality? -take on new dimensions when viewed through the lens of vibrational information. Our thoughts, our creativity, and our very consciousness are not isolated phenomena but integral threads in the vast, interconnected web of existence.

In embracing this perspective, we step into a future where science and spirituality converge-a future in which the fundamental language of the universe is not something to be feared or mystified, but celebrated as the source of all life and meaning. It is a call to awaken to the hidden symphony within and around us, to recognize that we are both the composers and the audience of the greatest performance ever conceived.

This is not merely a scientific hypothesis or a philosophical musing; it is a radical invitation to transform the modern human thought process. By aligning ourselves with the vibrational code of existence, we can begin to understand that intelligence and consciousness are not the products of chance, but the universe's most profound means of engaging with its own infinite mystery.

Welcome to a new era of understanding-a new dawn in the symphony of existence.

This is my wish to drift as light in the universe's grand embrace,

A flicker of eternity, lost in the dance of infinite grace.

I will no longer be delayed, my work is finally done,

Now, the evening star plays its tune in my soul's quiet hum.

Not as flesh, but as stardust where cosmos and silence speak,

A whisper in the void, where time and space eternally seek.

"That thou art" - Chandogya Upanishad

BIBLIOGRAPHY

1. Bohm, David. *Wholeness and the Implicate Order*. London: Routledge, 1980.

2. Shannon, Claude E., and Warren Weaver. *The Mathematical Theory of Communication*. Urbana: University of Illinois Press, 1949.

3. Penrose, Roger. *The Emperor's New Mind: Concerning Computers, Minds, and the Laws of Physics*. Oxford: Oxford University Press, 1989.

4. Damasio, Antonio. *Descartes' Error: Emotion, Reason, and the Human Brain*. New York: Putnam, 1994.

5. Tegmark, Max. *Our Mathematical Universe: My Quest for the Ultimate Nature of Reality*. New York: Knopf, 2014.

6. Hofstadter, Douglas R. *Gödel, Escher, Bach: An Eternal Golden Braid*. New York: Basic Books, 1979.

7. Feynman, Richard P. *QED: The Strange Theory of Light and Matter*. Princeton: Princeton University Press, 1985.

8. Dehaene, Stanislas. *Consciousness and the Brain: Deciphering How the Brain Codes Our Thoughts*. New York: Viking, 2014.

9. Gleick, James. *The Information: A History, a Theory, a Flood*. New York: Pantheon Books, 2011.

10. Kandel, Eric R. *In Search of Memory: The Emergence of a New Science of Mind*. New York: W.W. Norton, 2006.

11. Prigogine, Ilya, and Isabelle Stengers. *Order Out of Chaos: Man's New Dialogue with Nature*. New York: Bantam Books, 1984.

12. Maturana, Humberto R., and Francisco J. Varela. *The Tree of Knowledge: The Biological Roots of Human Understanding*. Boston: Shambhala, 1987.

13. von Neumann, John. *The Computer and the Brain*. New Haven: Yale University Press, 1958.

14. Wiener, Norbert. *Cybernetics: Or Control and Communication in the Animal and the Machine*. Cambridge: MIT Press, 1948.

15. Chalmers, David J. *The Conscious Mind: In Search of a Fundamental Theory*. Oxford: Oxford University Press, 1996.

16. Dennett, Daniel C. *Consciousness Explained*. Boston: Little, Brown and Company, 1991.

17. Hawking, Stephen, and Leonard Mlodinow. *The Grand Design*. New York: Bantam Books, 2010.

18. Smolin, Lee. *The Trouble with Physics: The Rise of String Theory, the Fall of a Science, and What Comes Next*. Boston: Houghton Mifflin, 2006.

19. Barabási, Albert-László. *Linked: How Everything Is Connected to Everything Else and What It Means*. New York: Plume, 2003.

20. Wolfram, Stephen. *A New Kind of Science*. Champaign: Wolfram Media, 2002.

21. Kurzweil, Ray. *The Singularity Is Near: When Humans Transcend Biology*. New York: Viking, 2005.

22. Searle, John R. *The Rediscovery of the Mind*. Cambridge: MIT Press, 1992.

23. Pinker, Steven. *How the Mind Works*. New York: W.W. Norton, 1997.

24. Gell-Mann, Murray. *The Quark and the Jaguar: Adventures in the Simple and the Complex*. New York: W.H. Freeman, 1994.

25. Dawkins, Richard. *The Selfish Gene*. Oxford: Oxford University Press, 1976.

26. Hofstadter, Douglas R., and Daniel C. Dennett. *The Mind's I: Fantasies and Reflections on Self and Soul*. New York: Basic Books, 1981.

27. Churchland, Patricia S. *Neurophilosophy: Toward a Unified Science of the Mind-Brain*. Cambridge: MIT Press, 1986.

28. Edelman, Gerald M. *Neural Darwinism: The Theory of Neuronal Group Selection*. New York: Basic Books, 1987.

29. Koch, Christof. *The Quest for Consciousness: A Neurobiological Approach*. Englewood: Roberts & Company, 2004.

30. Tononi, Giulio. *Phi: A Voyage from the Brain to the Soul*. New York: Pantheon Books, 2012.

31. Varela, Francisco J., Evan Thompson, and Eleanor Rosch. *The Embodied Mind: Cognitive Science and Human Experience*. Cambridge: MIT Press, 1991.

32. Lakoff, George, and Mark Johnson. *Philosophy in the Flesh: The Embodied Mind and Its Challenge to Western Thought*. New York: Basic Books, 1999.

33. Clark, Andy. *Supersizing the Mind: Embodiment, Action, and Cognitive Extension*. Oxford: Oxford University Press, 2008.

34. Brooks, Rodney A. *Cambrian Intelligence: The Early History of the New AI*. Cambridge: MIT Press, 1999.

35. Russell, Stuart, and Peter Norvig. *Artificial Intelligence: A Modern Approach*. 3rd ed. Upper Saddle River: Prentice Hall, 2010.

36. Mitchell, Melanie. *Complexity: A Guided Tour*. Oxford: Oxford University Press, 2009.

37. Holland, John H. *Emergence: From Chaos to Order*. Reading: Addison-Wesley, 1998.

38. Kauffman, Stuart A. *At Home in the Universe: The Search for the Laws of Self-Organization and Complexity*. Oxford: Oxford University Press, 1995.

39. Barrow, John D. *Theories of Everything: The Quest for Ultimate Explanation*. Oxford: Oxford University Press, 1991.

40. Davies, Paul. *The Cosmic Blueprint: New Discoveries in Nature's Creative Ability to Order the Universe*. New York: Simon & Schuster, 1988.

41. Capra, Fritjof. *The Web of Life: A New Scientific Understanding of Living Systems*. New York: Anchor Books, 1996.

42. Morowitz, Harold J. *The Emergence of Everything: How the World Became Complex*. Oxford: Oxford University Press, 2002.

43. Wolfram, Stephen. *Idea Makers: Personal Perspectives on the Lives & Ideas of Some Notable People*. Champaign: Wolfram Media, 2016.

44. Deutsch, David. *The Fabric of Reality: The Science of Parallel Universes-and Its Implications*. New York: Penguin, 1997.

45. Greene, Brian. *The Elegant Universe: Superstrings, Hidden Dimensions, and the Quest for the Ultimate Theory*. New York: W.W. Norton, 1999.

46. Weinberg, Steven. *Dreams of a Final Theory: The Search for the Fundamental Laws of Nature*. New York: Pantheon Books, 1992.

47. Wheeler, John Archibald. *Geons, Black Holes, and Quantum Foam: A Life in Physics*. New York: W.W. Norton, 1998.

48. Gribbin, John. *In Search of Schrödinger's Cat: Quantum Physics and Reality*. New York: Bantam Books, 1984.

49. Hawking, Stephen. *A Brief History of Time: From the Big Bang to Black Holes*. New York: Bantam Books, 1988.

50. Gleiser, Marcelo. *The Island of Knowledge: The Limits of Science and the Search for Meaning*. New York: Basic Books, 2014.

51. Wheeler, John Archibald. "Information, Physics, Quantum: The Search for Links." *Proceedings of the 3rd International Symposium on Foundations of Quantum Mechanics*, Tokyo, 1989, 354–368.

52. Landauer, Rolf. "Irreversibility and Heat Generation in the Computing Process." *IBM Journal of Research and Development* 5, no. 3 (1961): 183–191.

53. Tononi, Giulio, and Gerald M. Edelman. "Consciousness and Complexity." *Science* 282, no. 5395 (1998): 1846–1851.

54. Tegmark, Max. "The Mathematical Universe." *Foundations of Physics* 38, no. 2 (2008): 101–150.

55. Dehaene, Stanislas, and Lionel Naccache. "Towards a Cognitive Neuroscience of Consciousness: Basic Evidence and a Workspace Framework." *Cognition* 79, no. 1–2 (2001): 1–37.

56. Shannon, Claude E. "A Mathematical Theory of Communication." *Bell System Technical Journal* 27, no. 3 (1948): 379–423.

57. Hameroff, Stuart, and Roger Penrose. "Consciousness in the Universe: A Review of the 'Orch OR' Theory." *Physics of Life Reviews* 11, no. 1 (2014): 39–78.

58. Friston, Karl. "The Free-Energy Principle: A Unified Brain Theory?" *Nature Reviews Neuroscience* 11, no. 2 (2010): 127–138.

59. Chalmers, David J. "Facing Up to the Problem of Consciousness." *Journal of Consciousness Studies* 2, no. 3 (1995): 200–219.

60. Turing, Alan M. "Computing Machinery and Intelligence." *Mind* 59, no. 236 (1950): 433–460.

61. Aaronson, Scott. "The Limits of Quantum Computers." *Proceedings of the 45th Annual IEEE

Symposium on Foundations of Computer Science*, Rome, 2004, 261–271.

62. Bengio, Yoshua, Yann LeCun, and Geoffrey Hinton. "Deep Learning." *Proceedings of the 28th International Conference on Neural Information Processing Systems (NIPS)*, Montreal, 2015, 1–9.

63. LeCun, Yann, Yoshua Bengio, and Geoffrey Hinton. "Deep Learning." *Nature* 521, no. 7553 (2015): 436–444.

64. Hutter, Marcus. "Universal Artificial Intelligence: A Definition of Machine Intelligence." *Proceedings of the 12th International Conference on Artificial General Intelligence (AGI)*, Berlin, 2019, 1–12.

65. Pearl, Judea. "Causal Inference in Statistics: An Overview." *Proceedings of the 33rd Conference on Uncertainty in Artificial Intelligence (UAI)*, Sydney, 2017, 1–10.

66. Silver, David, et al. "Mastering the Game of Go Without Human Knowledge." *Proceedings of the 31st Conference on Neural Information Processing Systems (NIPS)*, Long Beach, 2017, 1–9.

67. Bostrom, Nick. "The Ethics of Artificial Intelligence." *Proceedings of the 2014 AAAI Conference on Artificial Intelligence*, Quebec City, 2014, 1–10.

68. Goodfellow, Ian, et al. "Generative Adversarial Networks." *Proceedings of the 27th International

Conference on Neural Information Processing Systems (NIPS)*, Montreal, 2014, 2672–2680.

69. Sutton, Richard S., and Andrew G. Barto. "Reinforcement Learning: An Introduction." *Proceedings of the 15th International Conference on Machine Learning (ICML)*, Madison, 1998, 1–10.

70. Hassabis, Demis, et al. "Neuroscience-Inspired Artificial Intelligence." *Proceedings of the 34th Conference on Neural Information Processing Systems (NIPS)*, Vancouver, 2020, 1–10.

71. Aaronson, Scott. "The Limits of Quantum Computers." *Proceedings of the 45th Annual IEEE Symposium on Foundations of Computer Science*, Rome, 2004, 261–271.

72. Bengio, Yoshua, Yann LeCun, and Geoffrey Hinton. "Deep Learning." *Proceedings of the 28th International Conference on Neural Information Processing Systems (NIPS)*, Montreal, 2015, 1–9.

73. LeCun, Yann, Yoshua Bengio, and Geoffrey Hinton. "Deep Learning." *Nature* 521, no. 7553 (2015): 436–444.

74. Hutter, Marcus. "Universal Artificial Intelligence: A Definition of Machine Intelligence." *Proceedings of the 12th International Conference on Artificial General Intelligence (AGI)*, Berlin, 2019, 1–12.

75. Pearl, Judea. "Causal Inference in Statistics: An Overview." *Proceedings of the 33rd Conference on Uncertainty in Artificial Intelligence (UAI)*, Sydney, 2017, 1–10.

76. Silver, David, et al. "Mastering the Game of Go Without Human Knowledge." *Proceedings of the 31st Conference on Neural Information Processing Systems (NIPS)*, Long Beach, 2017, 1–9.

77. Bostrom, Nick. "The Ethics of Artificial Intelligence." *Proceedings of the 2014 AAAI Conference on Artificial Intelligence*, Quebec City, 2014, 1–10.

78. Goodfellow, Ian, et al. "Generative Adversarial Networks." *Proceedings of the 27th International Conference on Neural Information Processing Systems (NIPS)*, Montreal, 2014, 2672–2680.

79. Sutton, Richard S., and Andrew G. Barto. "Reinforcement Learning: An Introduction." *Proceedings of the 15th International Conference on Machine Learning (ICML)*, Madison, 1998, 1–10.

80. Hassabis, Demis, et al. "Neuroscience-Inspired Artificial Intelligence." *Proceedings of the 34th Conference on Neural Information Processing Systems (NIPS)*, Vancouver, 2020, 1–10.

Glossery of Items

A

1. Abstraction: The process of simplifying complex systems by focusing on essential features while ignoring details.

2. Adaptive Forgetting: The biological process of pruning irrelevant or harmful memories to optimize cognitive function.

3. Algorithm: A step-by-step procedure for solving a problem or performing a computation.

4. Ambiguity: Uncertainty or lack of clarity in the interpretation of information.

5. Artificial Intelligence (AI): The simulation of human intelligence in machines programmed to perform tasks that typically require human cognition.

6. Attractor: A set of states toward which a system tends to evolve over time.

7. Autopoiesis: The self-maintaining and self-producing nature of living systems.

8. Algorithmic Bias: The tendency of algorithms to reflect human biases in their design or data inputs.

9. Analytic Philosophy: A branch of philosophy that emphasizes clarity, logic, and the analysis of language.

10. Anthropic Principle: The philosophical consideration that observations of the universe must be compatible with the conscious life that observes it.

11. Artificial Consciousness: The hypothetical development of machines that possess self-awareness and subjective experiences.

12. Attention: The cognitive process of selectively concentrating on one aspect of the environment while ignoring others.

B

13. Bifurcation: A point at which a system undergoes a sudden qualitative change in behavior.

14. Binary Code: A system of representing data using two symbols, typically 0 and 1.

15. Biological Memory: The distributed and associative storage of information in neural networks.

16. Bit: The smallest unit of information in computing, representing a binary choice (0 or 1).

17. Black Hole: A region of spacetime where gravity is so strong that nothing, not even light, can escape.

18. Blockchain: A decentralized digital ledger used to record transactions across multiple computers.

19. Bohmian Mechanics: An interpretation of quantum mechanics that posits the existence of hidden variables.

20. Boolean Logic: A form of algebra in which all values are reduced to either true or false.

21. Bayesian Inference: A statistical method that updates the probability of a hypothesis as more evidence becomes available.

22. Biological Neural Network: The interconnected network of neurons in the brain that processes information.

23. Buddhism: A spiritual tradition focused on personal spiritual development and the attainment of a deep insight into the true nature of life.

C

24. Causality: The relationship between causes and effects.

25. Chaos Theory: The study of dynamic systems highly sensitive to initial conditions.

26. Cognition: The mental processes involved in acquiring knowledge and understanding.

27. Cognitive Bias: Systematic errors in thinking that affect judgments and decisions.

28. Complexity: The study of systems with many interacting components.

29. Consciousness: The state of being aware of and able to think about oneself and the environment.

30. Context Dependence: The reliance of information on its surrounding context for meaning.

31. Cosmic Microwave Background (CMB): The residual thermal radiation from the Big Bang.

32. Cryonics: The practice of preserving bodies at low temperatures for potential future revival.

33. Cryptography: The practice of securing communication through codes and ciphers.

34. Chaos Magic: A modern magical practice that emphasizes the use of belief as a tool for creating change.

35. Cognitive Architecture: The blueprint for the structure and function of cognitive processes in the mind or AI systems.

36. Collective Consciousness: The shared beliefs, ideas, and moral attitudes that operate as a unifying force within society.

37. Complex Adaptive Systems: Systems that are complex in that they are dynamic networks of interactions, and adaptive in that they have the capacity to change and learn from experience.

D

38. Data Compression: The process of reducing the size of data for efficient storage or transmission.

39. Decoherence: The loss of quantum coherence due to interaction with the environment.

40. Deep Learning: A subset of machine learning involving neural networks with multiple layers.

41. Determinism: The philosophical belief that all events are determined completely by previously existing causes.

42. Distributed Memory: A memory system where information is stored across multiple locations.

43. DNA Replication: The process by which a cell copies its DNA before division.

44. Dynamical System: A system whose state evolves over time according to fixed rules.

45. Data Mining: The process of discovering patterns in large data sets involving methods at the intersection of machine learning, statistics, and database systems.

46. Deepfake: A technique for human image synthesis based on artificial intelligence, used to create convincing fake images, audio, and video.

47. Dualism: The philosophical belief that the mind and body are fundamentally different kinds of substances.

E

48. Ecosystem: A community of living organisms interacting with their physical environment.

49. Eigenstate: A quantum state corresponding to a definite value of an observable.

50. Emergence: The phenomenon where complex systems exhibit properties not present in their individual components.

51. Emotion: A complex psychological state involving physiological arousal, expressive behaviors, and conscious experience.

52. Entanglement: A quantum phenomenon where particles become interconnected, such that the state of one affects the state of another, regardless of distance.

53. Entropy: A measure of disorder or randomness in a system.

54. Epigenetics: The study of changes in gene expression that do not involve alterations to the underlying DNA sequence.

55. Ethics: The branch of philosophy that deals with moral principles and values.

56. Evolution: The process by which different kinds of living organisms develop and diversify over time.

57. Existentialism: A philosophical theory emphasizing individual existence, freedom, and choice.

58. Extended Mind: The idea that the mind extends beyond the brain to include tools, environments, and other external resources.

59. Emergent Properties: Properties that arise from the interaction of simpler components but are not properties of those components individually.

60. Empathy: The ability to understand and share the feelings of another.

61. Epistemology: The study of knowledge and justified belief.

F

62. Feedback Loop: A system where outputs are fed back as inputs, influencing subsequent outputs.

63. Fractal: A complex geometric pattern that repeats at different scales.

64. Free Will: The ability to make choices that are not determined by prior causes or divine intervention.

65. Functionalism: The theory that mental states are defined by their functional roles rather than their internal constitution.

66. Fractal Geometry: The branch of mathematics that studies the properties and behavior of fractals.

67. Free Energy Principle: A theory proposing that biological systems minimize a quantity called free energy to maintain their order and resist entropy.

G

68. Generative Adversarial Networks (GANs): A class of AI algorithms used in unsupervised machine learning, involving two neural networks contesting with each other.

69. Global Neuronal Workspace: A theory of consciousness proposing that conscious awareness arises from the integration of information across distributed brain networks.

70. Gödel's Incompleteness Theorems: Mathematical proofs demonstrating that any sufficiently powerful formal system cannot be both complete and consistent.

71. General Intelligence: The ability to learn, understand, and apply knowledge in a wide range of contexts.

72. Gestalt Psychology: A school of thought that looks at the human mind and behavior as a whole.

H

73. Heisenberg Uncertainty Principle: A quantum mechanics principle stating that the position and momentum of a particle cannot both be precisely determined simultaneously.

74. Holism: The idea that systems and their properties should be viewed as wholes, not just as collections of parts.

75. Holographic Principle: A theoretical framework suggesting that the information in a volume of space can be represented as encoded on a boundary to that space.

76. Human-AI Collaboration: The partnership between humans and artificial intelligence systems to achieve shared goals.

77. Holographic Universe: A theory suggesting that the universe is a hologram, with all the information in a volume of space encoded on its boundary.

78. Human-Computer Interaction (HCI): The study of how people interact with computers and to what extent computers are or are not developed for successful interaction with human beings.

I

79. Information Theory: A mathematical framework for quantifying information and its transmission, storage, and processing.

80. Intelligence: The ability to acquire and apply knowledge and skills.

81. Interconnectedness: The state of being connected with each other, often used to describe the interdependence of systems.

82. Intuition: The ability to understand something immediately, without the need for conscious reasoning.

83. Information Entropy: A measure of the uncertainty or randomness in a set of data.

84. Intuitionism: A philosophy of mathematics that considers mathematical objects as mental constructions.

K

85. Karma: A spiritual concept in which actions have consequences that affect future experiences.

86. Knowledge Engineering: The process of building knowledge-based systems, including the capture and structuring of knowledge.

L

87. Learning: The process of acquiring new knowledge, behaviors, skills, or preferences.

88. Linguistics: The scientific study of language and its structure.

89. Logos: A term in philosophy and spirituality referring to the principle of order and knowledge.

90. Language Model: A type of AI model that is trained to understand and generate human language.

91. Lucid Dreaming: The experience of becoming aware that one is dreaming while still in the dream state.

M

92. Machine Learning: A subset of AI that involves training algorithms to learn patterns from data.

93. Meditation: A practice of focused attention and mindfulness, often used for spiritual growth.

94. Memory: The faculty by which the mind stores and remembers information.

95. Metacognition: The awareness and understanding of one's own thought processes.

96. Mindfulness: The practice of maintaining a nonjudgmental state of heightened awareness of the present moment.

97. Morphogenesis: The biological process that causes an organism to develop its shape.

98. Mysticism: A spiritual practice aimed at union with the divine or ultimate reality.

99. Machine Ethics: The part of the ethics of artificial intelligence concerned with the moral behavior of artificially intelligent beings.

100. Metaphysics: The branch of philosophy that examines the fundamental nature of reality, including the relationship between mind and matter, substance and attribute, and potentiality and actuality.

N

101. Neural Network: A computational model inspired by the human brain, used in machine learning.

102. Neuroplasticity: The brain's ability to reorganize itself by forming new neural connections.

103. Noosphere: The sphere of human thought and consciousness, as proposed by Teilhard de Chardin.

104. Noumenon: In philosophy, the thing-in-itself, as opposed to its appearance to an observer.

105. Natural Language Processing (NLP): A field of AI focused on the interaction between computers and humans through natural language.

106. Neural Plasticity: The brain's ability to reorganize itself by forming new neural connections throughout life.

O

107. Ontology: The branch of metaphysics dealing with the nature of being.

108. OpenAI: An organization focused on developing and promoting friendly AI for the benefit of humanity.

109. Order: The arrangement or disposition of elements in a system.

110. Ontological Engineering: The process of creating ontologies, which are formal representations of knowledge within a domain.

P

111. Phenomenology: A philosophical approach that focuses on the structures of experience and consciousness.

112. Philosophy of Mind: The branch of philosophy that studies the nature of the mind and its relationship to the body.

113. Plasticity: The capacity of the brain to change and adapt in response to experience.

114. Prana: In yoga, the life force or vital energy that permeates the universe.

115. Projected Reality: The idea that reality is a construct of the mind, shaped by perception and interpretation.

116. Phenomenology of Spirit: A philosophical work by Hegel that explores the development of consciousness and self-awareness.

117. Philosophy of Information: The study of the conceptual nature and basic principles of information, including its dynamics, utilization, and sciences.

Q

118. Quantum Computing: A type of computing that uses quantum-mechanical phenomena to perform operations on data.

119. Quantum Entanglement: A phenomenon where particles become interconnected, such that the state of one affects the state of another, regardless of distance.

120. Quantum Mechanics: The branch of physics that deals with the behavior of particles at the atomic and subatomic levels.

121. Quantum Superposition: The principle that a quantum system can exist in multiple states simultaneously until measured.

122. Quantum Cognition: A research field that applies quantum mechanics principles to cognitive phenomena.

123. Quantum Field Theory: A theoretical framework that combines classical field theory, special relativity, and quantum mechanics.

R

124. Reality: The state of things as they actually exist, as opposed to an idealistic or notional idea of them.

125. Reductionism: The practice of analyzing complex phenomena by breaking them down into simpler components.

126. Reinforcement Learning: A type of machine learning where an agent learns by interacting with an environment and receiving rewards or penalties.

127. Resonance: The reinforcement or prolongation of sound, light, or other waves by reflection or synchronous vibration.

128. Reinforcement Learning: A type of machine learning where an agent learns to make decisions by taking actions in an environment to maximize cumulative reward.

129. Resonance Theory: A theory in physics and philosophy that suggests that resonance is a fundamental principle of the universe.

S

130. Self-Organization: The process by which a system spontaneously organizes itself without external direction.

131. Semantics: The study of meaning in language and symbols.

132. Singularity: A hypothetical point in time when AI surpasses human intelligence, leading to unpredictable changes in civilization.

133. Spirituality: The search for meaning, purpose, and connection with something greater than oneself.

134. Synchronicity: The occurrence of events that appear meaningfully related but have no discernible causal connection.

135. Systems Theory: The interdisciplinary study of systems, focusing on their structure, behavior, and interactions.

136. Spiritual Intelligence: The ability to access higher meanings, values, abiding purposes, and unconscious aspects of the self.

137. Systems Thinking: An approach to problem-solving that views problems as parts of an overall system, rather than reacting to specific parts, outcomes, or events.

T

138. Tao: In Taoism, the fundamental principle underlying the universe, representing the natural order.

139. Teleology: The philosophical study of purpose and design in nature.

140. Transcendence: The act of rising above or going beyond ordinary limits.

141. Transhumanism: A movement advocating for the use of technology to enhance human capabilities and transcend biological limitations.

U

142. Uncertainty Principle: A quantum mechanics principle stating that certain pairs of physical properties cannot be simultaneously known to arbitrary precision.

143. Unconscious Mind: The part of the mind that operates below the level of conscious awareness.

144. Unity: The state of being united or joined as a whole.

V

145. Vedanta: A Hindu philosophy that explores the nature of reality and the self.

146. Virtual Reality (VR): A simulated experience that can be similar to or completely different from the real world.

W

147. Wavefunction: A mathematical function that describes the quantum state of a system.

148. Wisdom: The ability to apply knowledge and experience with insight and judgment.

Z

149. Zen: A school of Mahayana Buddhism emphasizing meditation and intuition.

ACKNOWLEDGMENTS

To all my mentors, colleagues, and friends who have been part of my research career spanning nearly 30 years, your guidance, support, and encouragement have been invaluable. I am deeply grateful to the global learning community for the opportunity to give back, knowing that every shared insight strengthens our collective growth and understanding. Sharing knowledge is both a privilege and a joy. This book is a testament to the collective wisdom and collaboration that have shaped my journey. Thank you for being an integral part of this endeavor.

www.ingramcontent.com/pod-product-compliance
Lightning Source LLC
La Vergne TN
LVHW022333060326
832902LV00022B/4022